SATHYA SAI SPEAKS

VOLUME IX

(Revised and Enlarged Edition)

Discourses of

BHAGAVAN SHRI SATHYA SAI BAABA

delivered during 1969

SHRI SATHYA SAI BOOKS & PUBLICATIONS TRUST

Prashaanthi Nilayam - 515 134.

Ananthapur District, Andhra Pradesh, India

International Standard Book No. 81-7208-157-X
81-7208-118-9 (SET)

Published in India by
The Convenor, Shri Sathya Sai Books & Publications Trust
Prashaanthi Nilayam, India, Pin Code 515 134
Phone : 2175. STD : 08555. ISD : 91-08555. Fax : 08555-2190

Price : Rs. 20.50

Printed by
SRIKALS GRAPHICS
19, Kitabath Khan Bahadur Street
Ellis Road, Madras 600 002
Phone : 848019

Contents

Publisher's Note

"SATHYA SAI SPEAKS" Series is, according to late Prof. N. Kasturi, the original translator and compiler, "a fragrant boquet of flowers that never fade or falter". These discourses were delivered by Swaami out of profound compassion towards seekers of Truth during the last few decades.

The need for revised and enlarged editions of the Scrics was strongly felt and expressed by devotees, especially by foreigners. An attempt has therefore been made in these volumes to meet their needs. The discourses have been presented year-wise so that there is no overlapping of the discourses delivered in a year, in more than one volume pertaining to the same calendar year. This rearrangement has resulted in an increase in the number of volumes, from the previous twelve to the present fifteen volumes, covering the years 1953 to 1982. Further new volumes will also be added in due course, to cover the discourses delivered after 1982.

The retention of Sanskrit words on page after page, in the previous volumes, without their English equivalents in most cases, was causing great confusion to readers, especially foreigners, who were not familiar with Sanskrit. In the present revised volumes, an attempt has been made to aid easy reading by replacing Sanskrit words with English equivalents wherever they do not affect Baaba's original expression. Sanskrit words have been retained wherever it was felt necessary to preserve the essence of the original expression of Baaba and where the English equivalents may not do full justice to the text in the particular context. However, in all such places the English equivalents have been given along with the Sanskrit words. Some very commonly understood Sanskrit words or Sanskrit words which are repeated too often are retained without English equivalents to retain the original flavour of Baaba's discourses. Further, in this revised volume, phonetic spellings have been adopted for all Sanskrit words uniformly to enable readers who are new to these words to pronounce them correctly and to remove any vagueness in the pronunciation of these words.

A Glossary has been added in these revised editions to provide comprehensive and detailed explanation of the more important Sanskrit words for the benefit of lay readers who may be interested in *Vedhic* religion and philosophy. It is hoped that this will be of great help to devotees to understand more clearly the topics of Baaba's discourses covering a wide spectrum of *Vedhic* philosophy.

The revised series of volumes are being brought out in a larger format, Demy Octavo size, so that they can be companion books with other publications in private libraries. Computerised typesetting using a larger size of type, a more readable type face and better line spacing have been adopted for more comfortable reading of the books, especially by elderly readers. Very long paragraphs have been split into shorter paragraphs and suitable sub-headings have been added in every page, to relieve the monotony on the eye and make reading a pleasure.

Better quality paper, improved binding, dust cover with new design and foil printing and plastic cover have been adopted for the revised volumes for better preservation and durable shelf-life of the volumes.

With these changes, it is hoped that the revised and enlarged volumes of "**Sathya Sai Speaks**" Series, will be of great benefit to earnest seekers in spiritual realm.

Sathya Sai Speaks

Does Sai speak these words into avid ears and arid hearts? No!....It is our Mother that speaks, caressing, cajoling, crooning lullabies to relieve the pain, bless with bliss, *Mokshayishyaami, maa suchah!* Don't weep, she cradles us!

She leads us softly along the road, over pebbles, thorns. When the path is bitter, uphill, hard, she sings us through *Yogakshemam vahaamyaham*---our Mother speaks.

Does Sai speak these words into tingling ears and twinkling hearts? No!.....It is our Father that speaks, refining, revealing, reminding our Name to us, long forgotten, long begotten! *Abhayam Sarva bhoothebhyo!* Don't fear, He armours us.

Upward, onward; goodward, Godward---guides us, guards us. When the path is tortuous, twisted, He pulls us through. *Na Shukhaa!---labhyathe sukham*---our Father speaks.

Does Sai speak the words into mazy ears and crázy hearts
No!....It is our Master that speaks, advising, admonishing,
Heating us crucibly, treating us crucially, leading to God
within.

Eessavaasyam idham sarvam! There's no two; He opens the
lid of Divine Box, with treasure encased in *koshas* five,
Sathyam, Jnaanam, Anantham Brahma....the Master speaks.

Does Sai speak these words into searching ears and seeking
hearts? No! It is God that speaks, stilling the mind of
waywardness, *Brahmavidh brahmaiva bhavath!* Become
and be, He wakens. "Dear wave! emerging; merge; dear
ray! run back," He calls.

"Dear spark! re-enter fire; You are I, I am you." *Soham* loses
sa sa and *ham; Om* alone is He and We, *Ekameva-aksharam
Brahmam*---Isness...*Om.*

This is how our Sai speaks.

N. Kasthuri

1. Alms and qualms

FROM this day of the Tropic of Capricorn, *Makara Samkramana*, as it is called, the Sun appears to move from South to North, and so, this Summer Solstice Day is celebrated as an auspicious festival, since ages. But, you must be concerned more with your own journey which is nearing its end with every sunrise. You are engaged in an incessant struggle with the Sun, to survive the onslaught of Time, which he measures with His steps. You yearn to escape the consequences of birth and the aftermath of death. You desire peace and joy; for this, you have to cleanse the mind so effectively that it is well-nigh eliminated. This is possible only when you identify yourself with the *Aathma*, rather than with the body, which is the casket of the *Aathma*, earned as a reward for one's activities of mind and body. When you live in the consciousness of the omnipresent *Aathma*, you live in love, love flowing and flooding in and through you, and all else.

1

Every morning, as soon as you sit up in bed, ask
yourself this question: "For what purpose have I come
into this world? What is the task set for me? What is
the triumph for which this struggle is preparing me?
Which is the grand victory for which I have to strive?"
You must have witnessed car festivals in the famous
pilgrimage centres. The colossal chariots of the temple
will be gorgeously decorated with flags and festoons;
stalwart bands of men will draw them along the broad
roads to the music of blowpipes and conches; acrobats,
dancing groups, chanters, minstrels, all precede it and
add to the exhilaration of the occasion. Thousands
crowd around the holy cars and line the streets. Their
attention is naturally drawn towards the
entertainments provided, but they feel happiest only
when they fold their palms and bow before the Idol,
installed in the chariot. The rest is all subsidiary, even
irrelevant to many. So too in the process of life, the
body is the chariot, the *Aathma* is the Idol installed
therein. Earning and spending, laughing and
weeping, hurting and healing, and all the various
acrobatics of daily life are but subsidiary to the
adoration of God, the attainment of *Aathma.*

Only yearning and anguish win God's Grace

The body is the chariot; *buddhi* (intelligence) is the
charioteer; desires are the roads through which it is
drawn by the rope of sensual attachments; *moksha*
(liberation) is the goal; *Moola-Viraat-Swaruupa* (the
primal-all-pervasive-Divine) is the Master in the
chariot. The car which you carry about has to be treated
thus. Instead, men are wildly milling round and round,
in dreary circles, from birth to death, pulled by wishes
or pushed by needs. No milestones on the pilgrim road

are crossed; no bridges are negotiated; no progress is registered. The very process of the journey is ignored.

You may say that progress is possible only through My Grace; but, though My Heart is soft as butter, it melts only when there is some warmth in your prayer. Unless you make some disciplined effort, some *saadhana*, Grace cannot descend on you. The yearning, the agony of unfulfilled aim melts My Heart. That is the *Aavedhana* (anguish) that wins Grace. How so many *Navaraathris* and *Shivaraathris* you may attend at this place, unless you illumine your heart and make it shine clear and pure, it will be shrouded in darkness, immersed in *raathri* (night) only.

Saadhana must make you calm, unruffled, poised, balanced. Make the mind as cool and comforting as moonlight, for the Moon is the Deity holding sway over the Mind. Be calm in speech, and in your response to malice, cavilling and praise. You complain that others are disturbing your equanimity; but, you do not know that though your tongue does not speak, your thoughts can unsettle the equanimity of those around you.

A person fixed in detachment is ever content

Detachment, Faith and Love---these are the pillars on which *Shaanthi* rests. Of these, faith is crucial. For without it, *saadhana* is an empty rite. Detachment alone can make *saadhana* effective, and Love leads quickly to God. Faith feeds the agony of separation from God; detachment canalises it along the path of God; Love lights the way. God will grant you what you need and deserve; there is no need to ask, no reason to grumble. Be content. Nothing can happen against His will.

I am reminded of Karna. In his last moments, he asked from the Lord just one boon: "I do not mind if you condemn me to be born, to face death in an endless cycle; only, bless me that in all my many lives, I am not constrained to stand before another, with hand extended pleading, 'Give'; and, bless me also that in all my lives, I am not constrained to send away a supplicant with the word, 'No'. Let not these two words, *dehi* (give) and *naasthi* (no) emerge from my mouth." A person fixed in *thyaaga* (detachment) and *yoga* (self-control) will never said *dehi* and can never hear the reply *naasthi*, for he is ever content, ever full.

Vivekaanandha was once asked by a cynical critic why he paraded his renunciation through the ochre robe. He replied, "This is no parade; this is a protection. I am wearing this ochre, because, seeing this, no one will approach me for alms or monetary help. And, so, that word 'No' which I am averse to pronounce need not be spoken by me. At sight of this robe, only seekers of salvation will come near me; for them, I have enough to give. I am moved when distressed people come near; but, I have no money to give them. This dress helps me to escape such painful situations." You should so regulate your life that these two words are not used by you, while you live.

No bird or beast is to be despised

Do not grieve, nor be the cause of grief. The very embodiment of *Aanandha* (God) is in you, as in others, as in all else. In spite of a multiplicity of containers, the contained is the same. That is the principle of *Sath, Chith* and *Aanandha* (Being, Awareness, Bliss). The minutest atom, the mightiest star---both are basically one. All are, in truth, *Brahman,* Divine. You read in the sacred books that *Vishnu* (God engaged in Preservation, Protection and Fostering the Universe) has as His vehicle, the *Garuda* (Eagle); that *Shiva* (God engaged in the Mergence, the Disintegration and Destruction of the Universe) has the *Nandhi* (Bull) as His vehicle; that *Brahma* (God engaged in the Emergence, Evolution and Creation of the Universe) rides on a *Hamsa* (Swan); *Subrahmanya* (the Generalissimo of the Divine army) rides on a peacock; *Shani* (the God who directs Saturnine influences) has the crow as his vehicle. *Ganesha* (the God who helps in overcoming obstacles) rides on a mouse, though he is stupendously corpulent and has the head of an elephant! This does not mean that the Gods are helpless without these animals and birds as instruments of locomotion. It only reveals that no bird or beast is to be despised; for, the Divine is using each as His vehicle. Seen as *deha* (body) all are distinct; seen as *dehi* (the embodiment), *Brahman*, all are One.

See the unity in the teachings of all religions

Saadhana (spiritual striving) will disclose to you this identity. But be careful; *Saadhana* can foster even pride and envy, as the by-product of progress. You calculate how much or how long you have done *saadhana* and you are tempted to look down on another, whose record is less. You are proud that you have written the name of Sai ten million times; you talk about it whenever you get the chance, so that others may admire your faith and fortitude. But, it is not the millions that count; it is the purity of mind that results from genuine concentration on the name. Your *saadhana* must avoid becoming like drawing water from a well in a cane basket! You get no water however often you may dip and pull the basket up. Each vice is a hole in the bucket. Keep the heart pure, keep it whole.

All religions exhort man to cleanse the heart of malice, greed, hate and anger. All religions hold out the gift of Grace as the prize for success in this cleansing process. Ideas of superiority and inferiority arise only in a heart corrupted by egoism. If some one argues that he is higher or that his religion is holier, it proves that he has missed the very core of his faith. Leaves, flowers, fruits---these may be peculiar to each species; but pay attention to the trunk, and you will find similarity emerging. *Saadhana* will reveal likewise, the unity in the fundamental teachings of all religions. It is, of course, a hard path; but, it is a path that every one has to take now or later.

The signs of success in meditation

There was a fellow who clamoured for *Moksha* (Liberation) the easy way. He approached a *Guru* and asked for the quickest means of attaining it. "Know yourself," said the *Guru*. "O, that I know. I am just now your disciple. So, have I the *moksha* I want?" he asked; but the *Guru* said, it was not so simple as all that. He was, the *Guru* told him, behind and beyond the body, manipulating the senses, the intelligence, the ego; he was the *Aathma*, in the very core of the five sheaths---the *Annamaya* (the food or physical sheath), the *Praanamaya* (the vital, the nerve-centred), the *Manomaya* (the mental, imagination-centred, symbol-dealing), the *Vijnaanamaya* (intelligence-centred, reason-based, logical) and the *Aanandhamaya* (intuition-centred, experience- based, blissful). The *Guru*, however, gave him a tabloid prescription: "Repeat the Name of God, from the heart, with yearning to visualise Him." He said, "If you remind yourself continuously of God being your innermost Being, this awareness will come to you in a flash, through His Grace." The fellow shied at this; he queried whether he cannot employ any one to do the repetition for him! At this, the *Guru* asked, "Do you employ some one to eat or sleep on your behalf? When you fall ill do you get someone else to swallow the drug or take the injection?"

You sit in *Dhyaana* (meditation) for ten minutes, after the evening *Bhajan* (devotional chanting) sessions; so far, so good. But, let me ask, when you rise after the ten minutes and move about, do you see every one in a clearer light, as endowed with Divinity? If not *Dhyaana* is a waste of time. Do you love more, do you talk less, do you serve others, more earnestly? These are the signs of success in *Dhyaana*. Your progress must be authenticated by your character and behaviour. *Dhyaana* must transmute your attitude towards beings and things; else it is a hoax. Even a boulder will, through the action of sun and rain, heat and cold, disintegrate into mud and become food for a tree. Even the hardest heart can be softened so that the Divine can sprout therein.

You come to Prashaanthi Nilayam, as cars come to a workshop. You must go out, with a new paint, with all the damaged and loose bolts and nuts replaced, with the engine cleaned and reconditioned, every part spick and span, beautiful, trouble free, in perfect trim, ready to speed on the journey that lies ahead. Every bad habit has to be replaced by a good one, no trace of vice must be allowed to persist, the heart must be drained of all egoism. This is the fruit of this pilgrimage that you must acquire. Let this be your resolution, on this *Uttharaayana* Festival.

Prashaanthi Nilayam, 13-1-1969

2.   *Charming saplings*

THE magnificent mansion that was created by the
sages of the past, for the peaceful and prosperous
existence of their succeeding generations, the
mansion called *Sanaathana Dharma* has crumbled
through the wanton neglect of the sons and daughters
of *Bhaarathmaatha*. Now, peace and joy are to be found
only among these little children, the elders have lost the
art, the discipline, of regaining them and retaining them.

These children are fresh charming saplings, who can
be made, by care and love, to blossom into ideal citizens of
this land, able to understand and practise the great
disciplines laid down by the sages for their liberation,
through self-realisation. The mother and the father must
bear a major share of the responsibility for the proper
upbringing of children. The earliest years of life are the
most crucial. The skills, the attitudes, the emotions, the
impulses that make or mar the future are built into the
Foundation of Life in those years. The parents can help or
hinder the making of that foundation, strong and

straight. But, the parents have no equipment now for this basic role. They have no faith in their own ancient culture; they themselves have no mental peace, no *saadhana*, no spiritual discipline, which the children can imbibe from them.

Children must grow up in homes, where their parents honour their parents, in their turn, and are happy only when they serve their elders. Then only will children revere their parents! This must be taught to them by example, rather than by precept! Schooling is a waste, if children do not learn lasting virtues, do not develop strength of character, as a result of the process. They must learn reverence for parents, teachers, and elders. Now, they learn a number of copy book maxims; but, they do not put a single one into practice in daily life. For, practice is present nowhere.

Plant the seeds of love in tender hearts

Even as children, they must learn the glory of God who is their inner Reality; they must understand that they are not the body, but, they are the one *dehi* (indweller), who is the *dehi in* all. Through *bhajan* (singing devotional songs) and through *shravana* (listening to tales of God's Glory), these elevating truths can be handed over to them by teachers and parents who are themselves aware of these and practising them in daily life. Learn your own news, before getting excited about the news of others. Learn the A B C and D of your own alphabet and then, you will be better able to guide others, in their learning and life.

Do not ridicule the children when they go to a temple or a sage and show interest in *bhajan* or worship or *dhyaana*. Many elders believe that there is time enough for such pastimes, after one has lived

for sixty years! People who spread this nefarious
doctrine are ruining the lives of their dear ones, for, they
do not condemn the wrong and encourage the right.
There are others who by their behaviour and habits at
home, in full view of the children inculcate the habit
of uttering lies, gambling, drinking, etc.

Plant in those tender hearts the seeds of love,
sympathy, truth, justice, charity, compassion,
repentance and self- control. That is the prime duty of
all who deal with children. When the father asks the
child to tell some one at the door that he is not at home,
or when he asks its brother to reply to a phone call, that
he has gone out, the vice of dishonesty is implanted in
the child. Do not burden the tender brains with all kinds
of lumber, information that can never be put to use, facts
that warp and twist truth, etc. Teach them only as much
as they can use beneficially and as much as can be of
direct help to them in their lives. Train character more
than brains.

The parents first and foremost, the teachers next,
the comrades, playmates and companions next, and
the various levels of society later, these shape the
character of the children, and the destiny of the
country. You must revere the teacher, so that the child
may revere him; the teacher too must become worthy
of reverence and aware of his high role. This school,
bearing this Name, has an unequalled responsibility
in this regard.

Shri Sathya Sai Convent School,
Raajahmundry, 19-1-1969

3. Mahaashivaraathri

MANY stories are told in the *Shaasthras*, to explain the origin and significance of the *Muhaashivaraathri* Festival. Bhaarath, the name for this land used from ancient times, means 'the land of those who have *rathi* (Love) towards *Bha* (Light or *Bhagavaan*). So, for the people of this land, all days are sacred; every moment is precious. The Ganga is holy from source to sea, but, yet there are some places on its banks, associated with some sage or temple, the confluence of a tributary, or a historical incident, which are revered more by generations. Such places are Hardwar, Vaaraanasi, Prayaag, Rishikesh. Similarly, among all the days of the year, some are marked out as holier, when a special effort is made by aspirants to contact the Source and the Sea, the Reality behind all this passing show. Some moments, as that during which the *Linga* (Shiva representation in egg-shaped stone) emerges from the *Avathaar* (divine incarnation), are held to be specially significant for the individuals witnessing it and for the world which is thereby blessed.

Some ascribe the holiness of the Day to the fact of its being the Birthday of Shiva, as if Shiva has birth and death, like any mortal. The story that it commemorates the salvation attained by a hunter who sat on a *bilva* tree on the look-out for animals to kill, and without any intention to worship, unknowingly dropped some of its leaves on a *Linga* that lay beneath, does not make clear why this Day is specially sacred. Another story is that this is the Day on which Shiva danced the *Thaandava* (Cosmic dance) in the ecstasy of His Innate Nature, with all the Gods and Sages sharing and witnessing that Cosmic Consummation. When He consumed the *Haalahala* poison that emerged from the churning of ocean and that threatened to destroy the Universe, the heat of the fumes was well-nigh unbearable, even for Him. So, Ganga flowed uninterruptedly on His matted locks; but, that gave Him only partial relief. The Moon was placed on the head. That was of great help. Then, Shiva danced the *Thaandava* with all the Gods and Sages. All this they say, happened on the same day and so, *Shivaraathri*, was held in comme-moration of this occasion.

Aim of all *saadhana* is to eliminate the mind

We have not only the *Mahaashivaraathri* once a year, we have a *Shivaraathri* every month, dedicated to the worship of Shiva. And, why is the *Raathri* (the Night), so important? The night is dominated by the Moon. The Moon has 16 *kalas* (fractions of divine glory), and each day or rather night, during the dark fortnight, one fraction is reduced, until the entire Moon is annihilated on New Moon night. From then on, each night, a fraction is added, until the Moon is full circle on Full Moon Night. The *Chandra* (Moon) is the presiding deity of the mind; the mind waxes and wanes, like the Moon. *Chandramaa-manaso jaathah*—Out of the *manas* of the *Purusha* (Supreme Being), the Moon was born.

It must be remembered that the chief aim of all *saadhana* (spiritual striving) is to eliminate the mind, to become A-*manaska*. Then only can *maayaa* (illusion) be rent asunder and the Reality revealed. During the dark fortnight of the month, *saadhana* has to be done to eliminate each day a fraction of the mind, for, every day, a fraction of the Moon too is being taken out of cognisance. On the night of *Chathurdhasi*, the 14th day, the night of Shiva, only a fraction remains. If some special effort is made that night, through more intensive and vigilant *saadhana*, like *puuja* or *japam* or *dhyaana* (ritual worship, one-pointed repetition & holy names, and meditation), success is ensured. Shiva alone has to be meditated upon that night without the mind straying towards thoughts of sleep or food. This has to be done every month; once a year, on *Mahaa-Shivaraathri* a special spurt of spiritual activity is recommended, so that what is *shavam* (corpse) can become *Shivam* (God), by the perpetual awareness of its Divine Indweller.

Linga is the Form Symbol of God

This is a day dedicated to the Shiva that is in each of you. From the Himaalayan ranges down to Cape Kanyaakumari, the entire land is resounding today to the authentic Declaration *"Shivoham" "Shivoham"* and to the adoration, *"Om Namasshivaaya."* Since thousands pray here, and elsewhere in lakhs and crores, the *Linga* is emanating from Me, so that you may derive the Bliss that pervades the World through *Lingodhbhava* (emergence of the *Linga*).

The manifestation of the *Linga* is a part of My Nature. These *Pandiths* (scholars of spirituality) explain it as

reminiscent of an epochal event in the past when Shiva
challenged Brahma and Vishnu to gauge the height and
depth of the *Linga* Form He assumed. They failed and
had to accept defeat. But, the *Linga* emerges, as a result
of prayer and Grace. You have to recognise in this event
a glimpse of Divinity, a sign of infinite Grace. Just as *Om*
is the sound symbol of God, the *Linga* is the Form symbol
or the visible symbol of God, the most meaningful, the
simplest and the least endowed with the appendages of
attributes. *Lingam* means, that in which this *jagath*
(world of change) attains *laya* (mergence or dissolution),
Leeyathe. All Forms merge in the Formless at last. Shiva
is the Principle of the Destruction of all Names and
Forms, of all entities and individuals. So, the *Linga* is
the simplest sign of emergence and mergence.

Live in the constant presence of Shiva

Every form conceived in the *Shaasthras* and scriptures
has a deep significance. Shiva does not ride an animal called
in human language, a bull. The bull is the symbol of Stability
standing on four legs, *Sathya*, *Dharma*, *Shaanthi* and *Prema*
(Truth, Virtue, Peace and Love). Shiva is described as having
three eyes, eyes that see the Past, the Present and the Future.
The elephant skin which forms His cloak is a symbol of the
bestial primitive traits which His Grace destroys. In fact, He
tears them to pieces, skin them, and they become totally
ineffective. His Four Faces symbolise *Shantham* (Equanimity),
Roudhram (Terror), *Mangalam* (Grace) and *Uthsaaham*
(elevating energy). While adoring the *Lingam* on this
Lingodhbhava Day, you must contemplate on these truths of
Shiva that the *Linga* represents.

It is not this night alone that you should spend in
the thought of Shiva; your whole life must be lived in
the constant presence of the Lord. Endeavour: that is

the main thing; that is the inescapable consummation for all mortals. Even those who deny God will have to tread the pilgrim road, melting their hearts out in tears of travail. If you make the slightest effort to move along the Path of your own liberation, the Lord will help you a hundred-fold. That is the hope that *Mahaashivaraathri* conveys to you. Man is called so, because he has the skill to do *manana*; *manana* means inner meditatio n on the meaning and significance of what one has heard. But, you have not yet emerged out of the stage of *Shravanam* (listening) ! All the joy you crave for is in you. But, like a man who has vast riches in the iron chest, but, who has no idea where the key is, you suffer. Hear properly the instructions, dwell upon them in the silence of meditation, practise what has been made clear therein; then, you can secure the key, open the chest and be rich in Joy.

Visualise Shiva as the inner power of all

You have given up even the little *saadhana* that *Shivaraathri* demands. In olden times, people will not put even a drop of water on their tongues, this day. Now, that rigour is gone. They used to keep vigil at night, the entire night, without a wink of sleep, repeating *Om Namasshivaaya* without intermission. Now, the name Shiva, is on no one's tongue. But, those who deny God are only denying themselves and their glory. All have Love in them, in some form or other, towards some one or other or their work or goal. That Love is God, a spark of the God in them. They have *Aanandha* (bliss) however small or temporary and that is another spark of the Divine. They have inner peace, detachment, discrimination, sympathy, the spirit of service. These are Divine in the mirror of their minds.

Resolve, on this Holy *Shivaraathri,* in the Presence of Shiva Sai, to visualise the Shiva as the inner power of all. With each breath, you are even now, asserting *"Soham,"* "I am He," not only you, but, every being that breathes, every being that lives, everything that exists. It is a fact which you have ignored so long. Believe it from now on. When you watch your breath and meditate on that magnificent Truth, slowly, the I and the He (the *Sah* and the *Aham*) will draw nearer and closer, until the feeling of separateness will fade away---and the *Soham* will be transformed into *OM*, the *Pranava*, the Primal Sound, the Fundamental Formula for God. That *OM* is the *Swaswaruupa*---the Reality behind this "relative reality."

Shivaraathri Day, February 1969

*Anger turns a man into a drunken brute. The other impulses are equally vicious. Seek only salutary **karma;** eat only **saathwik** food---food that will not disturb the equanimity you earn through your saadhana. Do not break the even tenor of your spiritual practice. Remember how Raamadas never gave up his **Naama saadhana** in spite of jeers and jail.*

Sathya Sai Baaba

4. *Thieves or Masters?*

MAN is wasting precious time, ignoring his status among all living beings, his equipment for the grand spiritual pilgrimage to Divinity, and his one fundamental task: achieving liberation from the cycle of birth and death. The sages of the past have realised the value and dignity, the worth and responsibility, of human life and they have laid down disciplines like the vigil and fast on *Shivaraathri* Day, in order to inspire man and instruct him, on the upward path to God. *Shivaraathri* is a word that connotes the dual nature of man and his duty to discriminate between the higher and the lower. *Shiva* means *Jnaana* (the Higher Wisdom, the Unifying Universal Vision); it also means, the lasting, the timeless, and the beneficial, the holy, the auspicious. And the second word, *raathri*, means darkness of ignorance, the blind pursuit of tawdry pleasures, the bewildering will-o'-the-wisp of sensory joys. It also means the transitory, the fleeting; it connotes the maleficent, the inauspicious, the sacrilegious. So, the message of *Shivaraathri* is: discriminate between *Shiva* and *raathri*---the *Praana* (life energy) and the Body, the *dehi* (indwelling of spirit) and the *deha* (body), the spiritual and the material, the *Kshethrajna* and *Kshethra*, called in the Geetha as *Vibhaaga-yoga* (the *yoga* of discrimination between matter & spirit).

Relying on the merely literal meaning of the words, people wait a whole year for this particular holy day to come, in order to miss a meal and call it a fast, to miss a night's sleep and call it a vigil! The fast is called in Sanskrit as *Upavaasa* and it means something far more significant than missing a meal! It means (*Upa*-near; *Vaasa*-living) Living with, or Living near. With whom? Near whom? Near and with God. *Upavaasa* means living in the unbroken constant presence of the Lord, by *Naamansmarana* (remembrance of Divinity); that is the real fast, holding fast to Him.

Understand the main purpose of holy days

And, *Jaagarana* (Vigil) ! It means keeping awake, shaking off the sleep of the senses and being fully aware of the Light of Love, that is the Divine essence, in all. It means, shaking off the drowsiness and laziness, and deep concentration in meditation and *saadhana*. Look at the word for heart in Sanskrit: *hrudhayam*. It means, *Hrudhi-ayam*, that is to say, "the divine heart"; the place where He resides, where He is installed. By vigilance and the practise of the constant presence of God, you must instal Him in your heart and see Him as installed in all other beings as well. That is the main purpose of these holy days and the regulations laid down for their observance.

Truth is basic principle of the God-ward life. It is emphasised in all the scriptures of man. Raama suffered exile in the forest for 14 years, in order to maintain the spoken word of his father; Dharmaraaja suffered exile for 12 years, in order to keep up the word he gave during the game of dice; Harischandra sold his queen and son into slavery, and himself became the watchman of a burning ghat so that he might keep the truth. These are the shining examples of the lesson of Truth, which the mother teaches her every child in this land. These holy days must be set apart for the contemplation of these great ideals.

Do not be false to yourself

The Sages addressed all human beings as "Children of Immortality, *Amrthasya-puthraah.*" But, in spite of this definite assurance and the inexhaustible joy that can be experienced therefrom, man degrades himself into an *Anrtha-puthra* (child of falsehood) and starts wailing that he lacks this, that or some other comfort or contraption! Thieves who rob him of valuable treasures, like peace and contentment, equipoise and courage, are being honoured as masters and masters who ensure peace and happiness are treated with irreverence and disgust. You can bolt your doors and windows against thieves, but, who can bolt the door against Death? The thieves---lust, anger, greed, attachment, pride and hate---are honoured as welcome guests and the real well-wishers like tranquillity and humility are shown the door!

You desire to drink a sweet drink, but instead of sugar, you drop salt into the cup, imagining salt to be sugar. That is the state of man, today. He craves for peace, but, does not know how to attain it. The means he adopts do not lead him to the anticipated end. A large percentage of people who come to me ask for *Moksha* (Self-Realisation or Liberation) from the bondage of grief and joy, birth and death. But, when I offer to bless them with the consummation of their wish, they do not come forward; they would rather have it, ten years or five years later. So, all the thirst and craving are just a pose; it is a fashionable slogan, and nothing more. Man must be sincere; his word must be in conformity with his feeling; his action must be in conformity with his word. Resolve on this practice, at least from today. Do not be false to yourself.

According to the practice on such holy days, the Prashaanthi Flag will now be hoisted by Me on this building. The Flag represents the spiritual victory of the *Saadhaka* who conquers the passions and emotions that drag him down and cultivates Love and Equanimity that elevate him. So, when the Flag goes up and unfurls on the Prashaanthi Nilayam you too must hoist It on your hearts and unfurl It there, so that It may announce your spiritual Victory.

Prashaanthi Nilayam, 15-2-1969

Do not calculate the length of time you have spent in the company of the Lord's Name, and exult. Calculate rather the length of time you have wasted, away from that contact, and repent. Have that name ever in your thoughts and you can brave any calamity.

Sathya Sai Baaba

5. *Love and reverence*

THE Glory and Majesty of the Lord is immanent in the Universe, as fragrance in the air, of heat in fire, or as butter in milk. He is the string that passes through and holds together all the beads. To know Him as such, to realise that He is the source, sustenance and *summum bonum* of all this Creation is the end and aim of human life. That is the sum and substances of the teachings of all the scriptures that man has inherited from the past, in all languages and in all climes. All religions are but essays at demarcating the path towards that consummation. All moral codes regulate human speech, action and feelings in order to enable man to see the path more clearly and to make his steps firmer thereon. India is the land where this precious knowledge was gained and spread by ardent seekers and sages.

But, today, we have to deplore the decadence of these ideals, and the downfall of Indians who have descended to the level of ridiculing the heights of spiritual bliss, these sages attained. The time has come now to revere the culture that granted them that vision and that victory, to rededicate yourselves to the pilgrimage towards Truth, to discover in the jungle of manifoldness the basic Unity, which is the reality. As equipment for this arduous journey, the sages have laid down various regulations, disciplines, practices and paths; by adhering to them, man is able to remind himself constantly that he is destined to realise his essential Divinity. The fast and vigil prescribed on *Shivaraathri* Day are examples of such disciplines; for, the fast and the vigil are intended to lead the mind away from the senses and towards the Lord.

Five *yajnas* to be done by every man

The sages have laid down, for the same high endeavour, five *yajnas* for every human being, wherever he may be, to whatever denomination he may belong. These *yajnas* are not elaborate ritual exercises, accompanied by *Vedhic* recitation, prescribed for the attainment of specific states of Bliss in after-life or specific victories of a worldly nature. They are simpler and more democratic. They are being performed, casually and without the awareness of significance, by man everywhere. These *yajnas* do not ask for complicated credentials from those desirous of doing them. Any one can enter upon them and succeed. They are indispensable steps in spiritual progress.

The five *yajnas* (sacrifices) are: (1) Sacrifice for God; (2) Sacrifice to propitiate the sages; (3) Sacrifice to propitiate the progenitors; (4) Sacrifice to propitiate the visiting fellow humans; and (5) Sacrifice to propitiate the animal com-panions. They are called *Daivayajna, Rishiyajna, Pithruyajna, Athithiyajna,* and *Bhuuthayajna,* in Sanskrit.

1. *Daivayajna* : It is commendable practice, the allotment of one small room for the shrine, while building houses. In every Hindu home, we have a domestic temple or

altar or shrine, where the members of the family, singly or all together, can adore God. Usually, there is a picture or idol placed there to remind them of the Vast Immeasurable which it represents. Daily worship is offered at this shrine, prayers are poured forth before it, meditation is done in that quietness, the Name of God is taken on the tongue and its sweetness enjoyed. This is the *Daiva-Yajna*; it purifies the household and brings God into the consciousness of man through all his activities.

Activities to propitiate the sages

2. *Rishiyajna* is the term used for the activities of man that propitiate the sages. They are mostly: the study and practice of sacred scriptures, that are the treasure of wisdom gained by the arduous asceticism of the sages. The *Vedhas* are the earliest, the most compendious, philosophically the deepest, texts, the most practical of all the scriptures, and the most universal. Then, we have the *Ruamaayana*, the *Mahaabhaaratha*, the *Bhaagavatha* and other narratives of the eternal struggle between right and wrong and the everpresent Grace of God which helps the triumph of the Right. These and other books cleanse and console, elevate and uplift, correct and convince, and fill the mind with courage and humility. It is indeed a tragedy that these vitalising springs of strength are neglected and people read, instead, books that are rabid and ribald, debasing and vulgar, describing the insane behaviour of demented unfortunates, without being aware of the harm they are causing to their own progress and mental health.

These books slowly bog man into the mire of sex and sin; they turn man back into bestial ways. Asserting that you are "men" is only half the task of life; one has also to prove through one's actions, speech and thoughts, that one is not a beast! That is the obverse of the first

assertion; it cannot be ignored. Be human; keep away the
beast; control your senses, passions and emotions with the
reins of discrimination and detachment. That is what the
good books teach. Go to them for counsel and inspiration.

Parents have to be cared for and obeyed

3. The third sacrifice is on behalf of your parents, the
Pithruyajna. The command of the *Vedhas* is *"Maathru
dhevo bhava; Pithru dhevo bhava"*---"May the Mother be
your God; may the father be your God." The stanza is
repeated ad nauseum today, but, there is no sign of
reverence towards the parents anywhere. A generation
that does not respect and foster its parents is bound to
end in disaster. Parents suffer great hardships, and deny
various comforts for themselves in order to put their
children through school and college; but, the children are
ungrateful; they taunt and tease, they cause mental pain
and physical hunger to their parents by ridiculing their
habits and attitudes, and dismissing their advice with
neglect. When the creators of your physical equipment
and mental make up are thus treated with sacrilege, how
can one expect you to adore the Creator of the Universe,
God who provides for all? Honour your parents, so that
your children learn to honour you.

There is a fine story mentioned in the *Puraanas*
about this. The Divine Parents, Shiva and Paarvathi,
once laid down a test for their two sons---Ganapathi and
Subrahmanya. They were to go round the whole world
and return to them; he who does it quicker will win the
prize. Subrahmanya started quick and fast, and was
pacing through highlands and lowlands; but, Ganapathi
walked quickly round the Parents and claimed the prize.
He said, the Parents are all the world---and the statement
was accepted as correct. Ganapathi was installed as the

Deity supervising the acquisition of knowledge and as the Deity who shall save all aspirants from obstacles on their path.

The moral of this story is that parents have to be cared for, and obeyed. That is the real *Pithruyajna*. They represent renunciation, tradition, the accumulated culture of the past, the permanent values, as contrasted with the fleeting vanities. That is the reason why *Shiva* is addressed as *Saamba-Shiva*, *Sa-Amba-Shiva*, *Amba* meaning Mother and *Shiva*, meaning Father, and *Sa* indicating *Sathya*, *Sarvavyaap* (Omni-presence), *Sarvajna* (Omniscient) and *Saakshaathkaara* (Self- Realisation).

Treat the stranger seeking food as God-sent

4. *Athithiyajna* means acts done to please and comfort the *A-thithi* (he who comes only for a day), that is to say, the Stranger, who comes to your door seeking food or shelter. Give him these, as an act of worship. Treat him as having been sent by God or as God Himself. This is a sacred task enjoined by the Vedhas. Share your meal with whomsoever asks for food when you are about to eat it. Appease his hunger before you appease your own.

5. The last of the yajnas is the *Bhuuthayajna*—steps to comfort and keep happy the animal collaborators and companions one has around him—bullocks, cows, goats, horses, which help you by their toil, and dogs, cats and other pets which make your home pleasant and full of joy. You should not keep them hungry or overwork them. If any animal depending on you for love and care sheds a tear in your home or farm, remember you will suffer greatly therefor.

Love and reverence—these are the real springs for sacrifice or *yajna*. Let all your acts, words and thoughts be filled with Love and Reverence. Then, you will have unshakable peace and joy.

Prashaanthi Nilayam, 15-2-1969

6. Japa, Saadhana

I AM told that you are *saadhakas* (aspirants of spirituality), and so I shall speak to you something about *saadhana* (spiritual practice). Well. What is *saadhana*, fundamentally? It is *'upavaasam,' 'upaasana.' Upa* means near, *Aasana* means sitting and *Vaasam* means residing. We sit near a cooler so that we may feel cool. We sit near God, so that we might derive some Godly qualities and get rid of ungodly characteristics. God is not an external contrivance or convenience like the air cooler. He is the *Antharyaamin*, the Inner Director, the Inner Reality, the Unseen Basis on which all this seeable world is built. He is like the fire-principle that is latent in wood, which can be made manifest, when one piece is rubbed vigorously against another. The heat that is produced consumes the wood in fire! *Sath-sangh* (Company of the good and the godly) makes you meet with other souls (individuals) of a like nature, and creates the contact that manifests the Inner Fire.

Sath-sangh means Meeting the *Sath*, the *Sath* which is spoken of while extolling God as *Sath-chith-aanandha*.

Sath is the Existence Principle, the *IS* that is the basic truth of the Universe. Align with the Truth, the *Sath* in you, the *Sathya* (Reality) on which the *Mithya* (false) is imposed by minds that do not see light. By dwelling in that Sath, the flame is lit, light dawns, darkness flees and *Jnaana Bhaaskara* (the Sun of Realisation) rises.

When there is hard rock below, you have to bore deeper for tapping the underground perennial pure water. The softer the subterranean soil, the quicker the success. Make your heart soft; then, success is quick in *saadhana*. Talk soft, talk sweet, talk only of God---that is the process of softening the subsoil. Develop compassion, sympathy; engage in service, understand the agony of poverty, disease, distress and despair; share both tears and cheers with others. That is the way to soften the heart, and help *saadhana* to succeed. *Sath-sang* is like quaffing pure crystal water. *Dus-sang*---the company of the vicious, the ungodly, the impure---is like quaffing salt water from the sea; no amount of sugar added to it can make it quaffable! It increases thirst.

Cultivate the Conscious of the One

Krishna is named *Yogeeshwara* in the Geetha. What does that mean? *Yoga* is defined by *Pathanjali* as the *nirodha* (control) of the *vritthis* (agitations) of the *chiththa* (mind-stuff). If the mind is stilled and free from waves produced by the wind of desire, then he becomes a *Yogi* and the Lord is the highest *Yogi,* for He is the ocean that is unaffected by the waves which agitate the surface. Krishna danced on the hood of the serpent Kaliya and forced it to vomit its poison, it is said. This is only another way of saying that he forced sensual desires to divest themselves of pernicious effects. *Yoga* of this type is the best means of attaining the *Yogeeshwara* (the

Lord of *yogis*); not breath control, but sense control is the prescription.

Transcend *anekathwa bhaava* (the consciousness of the many) and cultivate *ekathwa bhaava* (the consciousness of the One), that will end strife, grief, pain and pride. See all as but expressions of the same God, as appearances on the same screen, as bulbs lit by the same current, though of manifold colours and wattage.

Feel that you and they are able to talk and walk, think and act because of the God within. Differences that strike you while you cast your eyes are illusory; you have not yet developed the vision that makes you apprehend the unity which is the truth of all the seeming diversity, that is all! The fault is in you, not the world. The world is One; but, each takes it to mean what pleases him most! The world is One, but, each sees it from his own angle and so, it appears as if it has multiple faces.

There is both truth and travesty in the world

The *japamaala* teaches you the Unity, though it has 108 beads! If it is a *sphatika maala* (garland of crystal beads) you can see the string running in and through each bead, the inner reality on which all this is strung! If the beads are not transparent, you still know that the string passes through, holds together, and is the basis for the maala to exist! Why 108 beads? 108 is the product when 12 is multiplied 9 times, 12 is the number of *Aadhithyas* (Luminaries), that reveal the objective world, and so, symbols of the *Sakaara* aspect (the world of name and form, of manifoldness, the seeming variety, the fleeting pictures); 9 is the screen on which the pictures appear, the basis, the rope which deludes you as the snake in the dusk, *Brahman,* the Nameless, Formless, Eternal Absolute. 9 is the *Brahman* Number, for it is always 9, however many times you multiply it! It is immutable, for 9 multiplied by any number finally adds up to 9 only. So, when you turn the beads, impress upon yourself the fact that there is both truth and travesty in the world, that the travesty attracts, distracts and delights in deceiving you, diverts you into devious paths; the truth makes you free!

Now about the beads: Before everything you must know the symbolism of the fingers. The thumb represents *Brahman*, the eternal Absolute, the Immanent Principle. The forefinger, the index one, which indicates this and that, you and other, is the *Jeevi*, the Individual, feeling separate and distinct. When these two are joined at the tip, held in that position, it is the *Jnaana mudhra*, the Gesture of Wisdom, for, wisdom consists in the *Jeevi* becoming One with the *Brahman*, the Mergence of that which felt that it had emerged! The other three fingers, represent *Prakrithi* the Objective World, which is negated when the mergence is effected. They are the three *Gunas*, the *Saathwik*, the *Raajasik* and the *Thaamasik* (qualities of purity, passion and inertia), that by their interplay create the phenomenal world.

Japa must become the very breath of life

Hold the rosary over the middle finger, keeping the three *Guna* fingers together. This means that you are now transcending the world of attributes and qualities, of name and form, of multiplicity that is the consequence of all this transformation, and proceeding towards the knowledge of the UNITY. The Jeevi finger now slowly passes each bead towards the thumb (*Brahman*), touching the tip of the *Brahmam* finger when the bead passes over, so that the mergence is emphasised with every bead and every breath, for, while the fingers learn and teach the lesson, the tongue too repeats the *manthra* (holy formula) or the Name, with the *Pranava* (the primal sound of *OM*).

The *japamaala* (rosary) is very useful for beginners in *saadhana*, but, as you progress, japa must become the very breath of your life and so the rotation of beads becomes a superfluous and cumbersome exercise in which you have no more interest. *'Sarvadhaa sarva kaaleshu sarvathra Hari chinthanam'*---Always, at all times, in all places, *Hari* (the Lord) is meditated upon. That is the stage to which the *japamaala* should lead you. You should not be bound to it for ever, it is only a contrivance to help concentration and systematic contemplation. The belt has to be discarded when you have learnt to swim, the crutches when you are able to walk.

One can win *Guru's* Grace by earnest prayer

Be regular, in the beginning, in the hours you devote to Japa. On Sundays, when you have no worry of office or shopping, do more *Japam* until nine-o-clock in the morning. Do it with love and enthusiasm. It should become natural with you to do so. Of course the Grace of the *Guru* helps a lot; Vivekaanandha was sliding into atheism and agnosticism the more books he read, but a touch from the hand of Raama-krishna Paramahamsa transformed him completely. You can also win this Grace, by your efforts and earnest prayer.

Before you start *dhyaana*, your meditation session, chant *Soham*, inhaling So and exhaling *Ham*. *Soham* means 'He is I,' it identifies you with the Infinite and expands your Consciousness. Harmonise the breath and the thought. Breathe gently, naturally; do not make it artificial and laboured. It must flow in and out, soft and silent; if you have some flour on your palm and hold it near the nostrils, it should not get fluttered the least;

the breath has to be soft as that! The faster the breath, the sooner you are burnt up, the shorter becomes your life span! Slow breath quietens and calms the emotions. The mood of relaxation produced by this *Soham* recital is a pre-condition for a profitable session of meditation.

Other things are also needed for this relaxation : have no thorn of hate in your mind, develop *prema* (Love) towards all. Desire is a storm; greed is a whirlpool; pride is a precipice; attachment is an avalanche; egoism is a volcano. Keep these things away, so that when you do *japa* or *dhyaana*, they do not disturb the equanimity. Let love be enthroned in your heart. Then, there will be sunshine and cool breeze and gurgling waters of contentment, feeding the roots of faith.

Dharmakshethra, Bombay, 10-5-1969

> *Make your home the seat of virtue, of morality, of love. Control anger and greed. That is the sign of the genuine* **bhaktha**, *not unrestricted speech and movements. You may claim to be a devotee and declare yourself as such, when you speak; but, unless your egoism has gone and you love all equally, the Lord will not acknowledge your devotion!*
>
> **Sathya Sai Baaba**

7.   Cults and culture

SATHYA and *Dharma* are the two cardinal principles of *Sanaathana Dharma* (ancient but eternal spiritual code). They are the goals of all faiths, the teaching of all saints, the core of the achievements of all sages, the under-current in all scriptures. They spring out of the *Aathmathathwa* (essential nature of the Self), which is the lesson taught in the Geetha. The Geetha is the essence of the *Upanishadhs*, the *Vedhaantha* (the concluding essence of *Vedhas*). On the day when you are celebrating the anniversary of the Inauguration of *Dharma-kshethra*, it is necessary to remind yourselves of this. The *Vedhaantha* declares, '*Ihsaavaasyamidham sarvam*' (All this is enveloped by God), and so, how can man hate or deceive another? The rules and disciplines laid down in all religious systems have as their aim the application in daily life of this great Truth, the Immanence of God.

Sathya and *Dharma* (Truth and Righteousness) are the two eyes of every religion that has emanated from the primal *Sanaathana Dharma*: of Buddhism, Christianity, and Islam. They are further elaborated and exemplified in the epics and *Puraanas* of India. Raama entered the forests and suffered poignant agony for the sake of upholding *Sathya*. The Paandavas exiled themselves from their Capital and swallowed, unmoved, excruciating insults, in order that the cause of Truth may prevail. Harischandra reached the nadhir of grief and humiliation, but never gave up his hold on Truth! These are the models held before the men and women of this land for millennia, through song, drama, sculpture, painting, poetry and philosophy. They are beacons beckoning the people of all lands to a higher, nobler and more beneficial destiny. Nevertheless, today the children of Bhaarath are enticed by tiny titillating achievements, in the material sphere, won by western scientists and technicians, such as travelling in outer space or flying to the moon!

Might must ever bow to Right at all times

Consider the five Paandava brothers, immortalised in the *Mahaabhaaratha* epic by Vyaasa. The eldest is Dharmaraaja, born of *Dharma!* The second is Bheema, of the Mighty Mace. The third is Arjuna, the foremost bowman of the age. But yet, both Bheema and Arjuna yielded ever to the slightest nod of Dharmaraaja, for, Might must ever bow to Right. Transferring the story to modern times, we find that contemporary America is the Arjuna, Russia is Bheema; and both have to bow before Bhaarath, the Dharmaraaja, who upholds the cause of Right against Might, military, economic or other. What a great tragedy is it, then, that we who have to guide the world in the path of *Dharma* are ourselves losing faith in that path and straying into the riotous road of Power or Might!

The *Mahaabhaaratha* teaches other lessons as well. Let us turn to the opponents of Dharmaraaja, Arjuna,

Bheema and others. The uncle, who is leading the
cousins and their wicked brood against the Paandavas,
is Dhritharaashtra, the blind ruler. He has no 'Vision.'
Yes; the vision that only righteousness can confer! He
was blind, that is to say, he had no *Jnaana,* the recognition
of man's incompetence and God's Omnipotence. The
Paandavas made up for their inferior military strength by
faith in God's Omnipotence and their own impotence! And,
so, God Himself led them into the field and won for them
victory from the jaws of defeat!

Karma illumined by *Jnaana* brings about success.
Jnaana alone---the discovery that God is all---that alone
can win the Grace of God; self-effacement is the first
criterion of the *saadhana* that can save man from
bondage. Dhritharaashtra was blind, because, as that
name itself implies, he held on to the *raashtra,* held on
to all things that were not 'he'!, the real 'He,' that passes
from birth to death, and again gets born only to die,
unscathed. Everything that is not 'you' is an object; it is
luggage for the journey; the less of it, the more
comfortable the journey!

Dharmakshethra and Kurukshethra are within everyone

Dharmakshethra and Kurukshethra are not to be
looked for near Delhi or Hasthinaapur, on the map or on
the ground. Nor are the Paandavas and Kauravas merely princely clans figuring in the tale. The human body is
named *kshethra,* and so *Dharmakshethra,* is in every
one. When the owner of the body discards all desires, all
passions, all impulses and all propulsions, then the body
becomes *Dharma-kshethra!* A child has in its heart only
Dharmakshethra, for, it has not yet developed sensual
desires. It accepts whatever is offered. Its ego is not yet
ramified into the objective world of multiplicity. But,

later, when it grows branches and foliage, the *Dharmak-shethra* takes the shape of *Kurukshethra*!---the battlefield where the mind struggles between hope and despair, and is compelled to consume the diverse fruits, sweet and bitter, of one's acts.

The *Aathma* is described as a *Vidhyullekha* (a streak of lightning), of the splendour of a crore of suns! The word Geetha also means 'Lightning' and so, that *Vidhyullekha* is the Krishna in us, that is to say, the Geetha in us, the *Aathma* that is counselling us and correcting us, as the God within.

Do not throw overboard the *Bhaaratheeya* culture

Dharmakshethra, it was mentioned, is being developed as an International Centre for *saadhakas* and inquirers, eager to learn the *Sanaathana* (ancient) way of life. India has no dearth of temples and institutions claiming to guide the pilgrims to God. In a *Granthaalaya* (Library), only people interested in books will gather; the *Bhojanaalaya* (Boarding House) is frequented only by those who want a meal; the *Vaidhyaalaya* (Hospital) is resorted to only by the sick; but in the *Devaalaya* (Temple of God), we do not find today either devotees or God! This is the only House where the legitimate owner is absent! Temples were the centres for the spread of *Bhaaratheeya* Indian culture, and, when the attraction for western culture became strong, they were deserted, and left open to the ravages of time.

Everything is being judged with the American eye; American ears do the hearing for us! The American heart feels and fears, fancies and fashions our reactions to events and things. Of course, it is useful to learn from others. But you should not throw overboard the culture that has grown through the aeons on this soil, and fostered by the love of your ancestors, for your benefit.

How can the culture of America or that of any other country be congenial to Indians? Now the time is 7-30, evening. If you phone your friend in the States and tell him, 'I am off to a film show now,' he will reply, "It is 7-30, here too. I am off for my breakfast !" When it is morning here, it is evening there; when the sun sets here, he rises there. Time, climate, vegetation, temperament, ideals, the nuances of languages, folk ways, all take on a strange colour in a country that has had a different history. So, indiscriminate imitation will result in the loss of the peace that follows fulfilment. *Bhaaratheeyas* can get peace best through the folkways that have been prescribed by the folkmind of this land, as a result of centuries of observation, experience, trial and error.

Develop brotherly feelings for all

Bhaaratheeya culture has emphasised the valid ways in which one has to spend energy and money for service of the distressed, the diseased, the hungry, the illiterate, the ill-housed, the ill-clothed. It condemns the spending of energy and money for pomp, for vengeance, for competitive faction, for material triumphs. Wealth is to be held on trust and used for promoting the brotherhood of man and the fatherhood of God. This culture also lays down that nothing should be done to damage any one's faith in God or in his own self. Faith is a tender plant and it needs all the nurture that you can give.

My desire is that you should not censure other religions. Develop brotherly feelings for all. God is One; there are not many Gods, one for each tribe among men! Love is One; it transcends caste, colour and creed, if it has to be genuine. Truth is One; there cannot be two. For, two can only be One, occurring twice. The Goal is One; for, all roads must lead to the One God. Why then should men quarrel and fight over the Eternal and the Absolute?

Dharmakshethra has a great part to play. It is in Bombay, which is the stomach of Bhaarath. The Himaalayas are the Head and the Kanyaakumari is the feet. When the stomach is inefficient, the entire body suffers the consequences. So, keep the *Dharmakshethra* efficient and strong. Do not allow it to degenerate into a *Kurukshethra*; let not friction and faction raise their heads here. Let the high ideals of *Dharma* (righteousness) be upheld here. This is the real *seva* (service) I expect from you and through you. If this is done, our land will have peace and security.

Dharmakshethra, Bombay, 12-5-1969

Attachment causes pain and detachment results in joy. But, you cannot easily detach yourself from activity; the mind clings to something or other. Make it cling to God, let it do all things for God and leave the success or failure of the thing done to God, the loss and the profit, the elation or the dejection. Then, you have the secret of **Shaanthi** *and contentment.*

Sathya Sai Baaba

8. 'In it,' not 'of it'

THERE are in this huge gathering people speaking many languages. Each one man understand only his language, and wants that he should be spoken to in that language. But, there is a language of the heart, which all can understand and all would like to hear. That is the language which I speak, the language that goes from My heart to yours. When heart speaks to heart, it is love that is transmitted, without any reservation. The trials and turmoils, the throes and thrills, the search and sorrow---these are the same in quality for all mankind. The responsive heart listens to these with sympathy and answers with love.

Every one is eager to be happy; every one wants to work less and gain more, give little and get amply, but no one experiments with the other method, that is, wanting less and giving more. Every want is a shackle that hinders movement, that is a drag on the foot. A young college student can roam free on his two legs; when he marries, he becomes four-footed! A child makes him six-footed; the range of his movements is restricted. The more the feet, the less the speed, the tighter his grip on the ground; the centipede has to crawl. More things, more hurdles, more handicaps. Accumulation of sofas and chairs, cots and tables, shelves and curios clutter the hall and render movements slow and risky. Reduce wants, live simply, that is the way to happiness. Attachment brings sorrow in its wake; at last, when death demands that everything be left behind and everybody be deserted, you are overpowered with grief! Be like the lotus on water; on it, not in it. Water is necessary for the lotus to grow; but, it will not allow even a drop to wet it. The objective world is the arena of virtue and the gymnasium for the spirit. But, use it only for that purpose; do not raise it to a higher status and adore it as all-important.

God is visible when concretised by *saadhana*

There are people who go about declaring that there is no God, because they are not able to see Him. They say that they have searched in space, on the way to the moon, and even on the moon but there was no sign of the Almighty. But they themselves are, all the time, the mansions in which He resides! Like the blind bamboozling the blind into a fall, others too repeat like parrots this 'fashionable slogan." No one sees the roots, but, they are there, deep in the soil, away from all eyes. Can you, do you assert, that there are no roots for trees, that nothing feeds them or upholds them, from below? God feeds, sustains, holds firm---unseen. He can be seen by those who make the effort, along the lines laid down for the purpose, by those who have succeeded in experiencing Him. God is, as butter in milk, visible when concretised by *saadhana* (spiritual striving).

You do not see the foundations of a multi-storeyed sky-scraper. Can you, therefore, argue that it simply sits on the ground? The foundations of this life are laid deep in the past, in lives already lived by you. This structure has been shaped by the ground plan of those lives. The unseen decides the bends and the ends; the number of floors, the height and weight.

God is the great Unseen, the vast Unknowable. Though you do not see the roots or know how far or how wide or deep they are clutching the earth, you pour water round the trunk, so that it may reach them, is it not? You expect that when the roots contact the water, the tree will yield fruit. Recognise, similarly, that there is God, as the very basis of Creation; pray to Him, and He will shower fruit.

The chief means by which you detach your mind from distractions and attach yourselves to the search of God are *Yoga* (communion with God) and *Thyaaga* (sacrifice). *Kaama* (desire) has to be got rid of by *Thyaaga* and *Raama* (God) has to be secured by *Yoga*. Desire discolours the intelligence; it perverts judgement; it sharpens the appetites of the senses. It lends a false lure to the objective world. When desire disappears or is concentrated on God, Intelligence is self-luminous, it shines in its pristine splendour, and that splendour reveals the God within and without. That is the real *Aathma Saakshaathkaara* (Realisation of the Self).

I bless you that you succeed in the *Saadhana* in which you are engaged; if you are not practising any now, I advise you to take up the simple one of *Naamasmarana* (remembrance of the Divine), along with reverence towards parents and elders and teachers, service rendered to the poor and the sick. See every one of them as your *Ishtadhevatha* (the Lord in the Form you like most). That will fill your heart with Love and give you stability of mind and peace.

Ahmedabad, 15-5-1969

9. The tell-tale tongue

YOU are all at school; you are reading books, attending classes, and you all say, "We are students." Because, you are studying; studying many subjects. This study will help you to do some work or get into some job, when you grow old enough. You learn the ways of health, you play and do exercises to build your bodies firm and fast. This is very good; you must learn these things well. But, there are some other things, too, which you must learn to do, learn to do well. I shall tell you of those things today.

You must speak soft and sweet words to every one. Do you like the voice of the crow? No. You drive the crow away when it starts to caw; its speech is harsh, it is too loud for your ears. You must have heard the *kokil*, the cuckoo, haven't you? That bird looks very much like the crow; it grows in the nest of the crow, with the baby crows; it is fed by the mother crow, along with her own kids. But, no one will throw a stone at a *Koil*. Every one likes to hear its sweet voice. Speak soft and sweet; then, every one will like you.

The eye sees; the ear hears; the nose smells; the skin tells you if a thing is hard or smooth. The tongue tastes. These five are called *Indhriyas* (senses). Each of these five does one job, and is fit to do only that one job. The eye cannot hear or smell or taste; the ear cannot see or smell or taste or tell you if a thing is smooth or hard to the touch.

Two big jobs God has given to the tongue

This is not true of the tongue, for it can do two jobs, and not one. And both the jobs that God has given to the tongue are big jobs. Just think for some time about the first job---tasting! If a thing tastes bad, you do not like to eat it. Of course, if you are ill, you have to take the drug, even though the tongue says that it tastes bad. So, you should not spit out all things that tastes bitter. Some of those things help to cure your illness quickly and well. Remember another fact also; if a thing tastes nice, it may not be good for your health. The tongue tells you that a thing tastes bitter or sweet, or saltish. It cannot tell you whether a thing is good for you or bad. So, you must care not to eat too much and spoil your health. When the body is ill, the mind too becomes weak, and the brain cannot work properly.

Now, about the second job that the tongue is given---speech. It is a tool that you can use in order to give vent to your thoughts, your ideas, your feelings, your desires, your prayers, your joys, your sorrows. If you are angry, you use it to speak out harsh words very loudly. If you are pleased, you use it to speak soft words in a low pleasant voice. I want you to use your tongue only for your good and the good of others. If you speak harshly to another, he too talks loud and harsh; angry words cause more angry words. But, if you use soft and sweet words when another is angry towards you, he will calm down, he will be sorry that he used his tongue in that way. Do not shout, do not talk longer than necessary, do not talk when there is no need to talk; when you speak to some one or some group of friends, raise your voice to the pitch tha t is just right for the listener or listeners and not more. Why should you waste your energy to talk louder and longer than necessary?

Use the tongue for your good and good of others

Never use foul words against another. Such words should not rise from your tongue, nor should they enter the ear of the others. Remember that there is God inside your heart, as well as in the hearts of all rest. He hears and sees all things. Do you not say, "My head, my hands, my eye, my mind, my idea." Now, who is this I, that owns the body, the mind, the brain? That I is the spark of God that is in you. That spark is in every one. So, when you use harsh, cruel, angry, foul words against another, the God in you and the God in the other person is hurt. The tongue is a tool, as I said. You can harm yourself and harm others with it. So, be very careful; use it only for your good and for the good of others. If you use it for talking kind words, for repeating the Name of God or singing His Glory, or praying to Him---then, it is put to the best use.

I shall tell you something more about the tongue. You can learn much by watching the tongue. It stays in its own home and seldom comes out of its doorstep. It keeps quietly indoors; it knows its limits; it has no desire to wander or roam about. This is a lesson you should learn from it. Make yourself busy and useful at home; help your parents and brothers and sisters; do not run out into the street and move place to place, without aim or purpose. Do not rush into the homes of others and disturb them. The tongue never goes into

another mouth; it remains inside its own home. It is not
proper to leave one's home and waste time, standing or
sitting idly, gazing at all those who pass by. You must
earn a good name, at home and at school, by your strict
mode of life.

Watch around you to avoid accidents

Do you know of another lesson that the tongue is
trying to teach you? Watch your tongue when you are
reading aloud or talking to some one. It moves quickly
from one side to another, it moves forward and back, in
order that the breath can come out as different sounds.
And, when you are eating your lunch or dinner, the
tongue has to move about pretty quickly. Have you
noticed that during all this time, the tongue has to be
very careful not to come between the teeth? There are
32 of them, all around the tiny home, with sharp edges
like swords, which may cut into the soft thick tongue
and wound it, causing it to bleed. Yet, see how skilfully,
how cleverly, the tongue moves inside the mouth,
escaping the 16 pairs of merciless soldiers that are
looking out to wound it! You must also watch all round
you, so as to avoid dangers and accidents. Do not fall into
bad company, do not be led into bad habits, do not bring
a bad name to your parents or your school.

We can learn another lesson, too, from the tongue.
The tongue has no greed; it does not keep anything for
itself. It does not store anything secretly, away from
others' hand, so that it can have it all for itself. If a thing
is good, the tongue sends it down the throat, to the
stomach; if a thing is bad, bitter, or rotten, it sends it out,
beyond the lips, as vomit! It has no urge to have anything
for itself. It serves others; it puts its own needs last. It
does not even keep a trace of the things that pass over

it, on the way out or in. It may be oil or ghee, cream or jam; the tongue is as clean as before. It has no likes or dislikes; you must also give up greediness. Do not get too fond of any one or any thing. Do all your duties well; give full joy to your parents and teachers. Help all as much as you can. But, learn also to keep quiet for some time every day, and be calm when some thing happens in the way you do not like.

God will yield to your prayers and get bound

Some of you may know how elephants are caught and tamed. In the forests, the elephant is a wild beast, moving in herds and charging any one who dare go near. It is trapped, roped, and tied to a strong post, so that it cannot run away; it is made so tame that it stands on a small round three-legged stool, in the circus tent, or drags huge logs of timber, at the bidding of the mahout! When the elephant is tied to the post, all its strength and skill becomes yours, for you can use them for your own need. The tongue is a post; Bhajan of the Name of God is the rope; with that rope, you can bring God Almighty near you and tie Him up, so that His Grace becomes yours. God is so kind that He will yield to your prayers and get bound. You have only to call on Him, to be by your side, with you, leading you and guiding you.

Every one likes to keep what he has got; he feels hurt when some one takes it away from him, by force, or by cheating him. This is called theft. If your book or pen is stolen by another boy or girl, you will be very sad, isn't it? Do not make another boy or girl sad, by stealing her or his book or pen. Do unto others only as you would like them to do unto you. There is a song used in *Bhajans---Badaa chiththa chor*---where God is said to be a "big thief, who steals the hearts of persons!" The whole world is God's. All of you belong to Him, though you may not know it. Therefore, He can take anything from any one. He is the Master of the ether, wind, fire, water and earth; He can change the sky into the earth and the earth into the sky. So, He can take hold of the hearts of people and fill them with Love.

Once people know how great is the Love that God gives, they will not desire any thing else. That is why He is called *Chiththa Chor* (Heart-thief). When you sing that song, you must pray, "O God! Enter My Heart also, fill it with Love, so that I may love all your children, in all lands." Never take hold of what others own. Do not talk ill of others. Do not talk about others but, if you must, talk only of the good in them. All are good; if you see bad in them, it is because there is bad in you. If you do not like some one, do not mix with him; keep away. But, do not try to blacken his name, and relate stories about him to others. Anger is harmful; it makes you do things blindly. You will have to repent much for whatever you do in anger; when your anger cools down, you see things clearer and then, it is too late to correct the wrong you have done!

Anger makes you do things blindly

You must read good books. Then only you claim to be good students. But, good books are now becoming rare. Cheap books and magazines give stories of bad life, dealing with crooks and cruel men, cheats and dacoits. Keep away from such books; they will dirty the mind, and fill it with anger and hate, and mischief. Read the sacred books of your religion and of other religions. Read the *Mahaabhaaratha*, the *Raamaayana*, the *Bhaagavatha*, the Bible, the Quran and other sacred books. In some families reading of such books is done daily; so, the children know something about the sages, saints and Divine persons of the past. Such reading is not done in most families; even the elders do not know what the books have in their pages! How then can the children know?

When you ask a boy about Raama or Krishna, he answers, "O, he is a boy studying in the same class as mine." He does not know that Krishna was God come as man, to help all men to reach Him! He does not know that Krishna taught Arjuna the Way to God, and that the teaching is found in the book of verses called *Geetha*. He does not know that Raama was a great King, who lived as an example to every one, for ever. He was also God come down as man, to show man the Path to God. There are many paths to God, as there are many roads to a city or as there are many tracks up a Himaalayan peak, by which sherpas can climb to the top.

Try your best to make your parents happy

You will find at home pictures of God, kept in a special place for worship. In every home, however, there are living Gods, whom the sages ask you to serve and worship. They are your parents. They gave you life; you owe your health and happiness to them. They love you, they serve you, they give you as much as they can, and even more. Yes; they often take less food, so that you can have your fill. They try to save money through various means, so that you can be at school, or live in a hostel, or attend a festival or go on a school tour.

The sacred books want you to honour them and worship them. "*Maathru dhevo bhava.*" "*Pithru dhevo bhava*"---"Let your mother be your God;" "Let your father be your God"---that is the teaching. Yes; how else can you thank them? What else can you give, in return, than your Love and Service? Think of all the care, all the love, all the pain, all the hunger and sleeplessness they underwent and undergo for your sake. Be kind, be soft and sweet to them. Do not be rude and disrespectful. Try your best to make them happy; obey them, for they know much more than you do of the world and its dangers. That is the way to worship them.

The sages also say, *"Aachaarya dhevo bhava"*--- "Let your teacher be your God." For, it is the teacher who opens the inner eye and makes you aware of the wonder and beauty of the world around you. He tells you of the truth of stars and sky, he teaches you how to be healthy and happy, useful and peaceful. The father and the mother brought you here and helped you to grow and gave you into the hands of the teacher. The teacher makes you bright and cheerful, skilled and serviceable to all. So, honour him, obey him and treat him with a much respect as you give to your parents.

In the book, *Mahaabhaaratha,* you read of a great battle that took place between cousins: the Kauravas and the Paandavas. Right was on the side of the Paandavas; they were fighting for truth and justice. So, God was on their side, helping them to win. The eldest of the Paandavas was the Prince called Dharmaraaja. His grandfather Bheeshma and his dear teacher, Dhrona, had chosen the Kaurava side and were getting ready to fight against him and his four brothers.

When the battle began, Dharmaraaja remembered the rule *"Pithru dhevo bhava,"*---"Let your father be your God," and *"Aachaarya dhevo bhava"*---"Let your teacher be your God." So, he walked up to the camp of the enemies, and reached the tents of Bheeshma and Dhrona, who were bent on defeating him! He fell at the feet of the grandfather and the teacher and prayed that they should wish him well. At this, they became soft and sweet to him; their hearts were filled with kindness; they said, "Son you have done only right and proper things, God is on your side; you will win. We have to be on this side, as in duty bound. But, we bless you that you may defeat your enemies and get back your kingdom." See how Dharmaraaja got the blessing of his grandfather and teacher, by observing the *Dharma* laid down by the sages!

Have faith in God and in your own strength

You are members of Sathya Sai Baala Vihaar. You must shine as fine examples to other boys and girls. When you are at home and when some friends of your father come in, you must rise from your seat, talk politely and clearly, receive them gladly, and be nice towards them. When you have to talk over the phone, don't shout rudely, "Hello, Hello," to every one. Elders must not be addressed so lightly. Hello! Hello! is not polite; it is used only among chums. I would like you to say, *Om*. Then, even your parents and elders will learn to say, *Om*, from you. You must use some word that is specially Indian. Now, you learn only the ways of other lands and other people. At school, the first lesson is: "Baa baa black sheep, Have you any wool?" and the second, "Ding dong bell, Pussy is in the well."

Gone are the days when the first lesson was on Raama, Krishna or some great sage or saint. Getting to know about black sheep will make children black sheep; getting to know about the great and the good will make children great and good. Children of the Baala Vihaar are therefore told stories of Raama, Krishna and other Divine persons. Learn those tales and decide to live like them. Learn Indian ways, Indian tales, and be true Indians. That is easy for you, and quite necessary. For example, why say, "Good

Morning" or "Good Night." *Namaskaar* or *Namasthe* is
the Indian way, the really humble way. You must have
Bhaya, Vinaya and *Vishwaasa*---fear, humility and
faith. Fear of what? Fear of doing wrong, of falling into
falsehood. Humility before whom? Before elders,
teachers, parents. Faith in what? Faith in God, in your
own strength, in your own victory.

I want each one of you to grow into strong, steady,
straight persons. Your eyes should not seek evil sights;
your ears should not seek evil tales; your tongue
should not seek evil speech; your hands should not
seek evil acts; your minds should not seek evil
thoughts. Be pure, be full of love. Help those who are
in worse condition, serve those who need your help.
Then, you shall be worthy members of the Sathya Sai
Baala Vihaar.

Dharmakshetra, Bombay, 16-5-1969

*Keep all personal animosity away from
your conduct. Feel that you are kith
and kin of each other belonging to the
same family bound together by love
and co-operation. Live amicably, live
joyfully, undisturbed by faction and
hatred; for, some day or other, you
have to give up all that you hope to
gain through these factions and these
hatreds.*

Sathya Sai Baaba

10. The will to will not

THE mind flits fast from one idea to another; it fondles for a moment and forsakes the next. You may manage to keep your mouths shut, but it is next to impossible to keep the mind shut. Mind is of that nature; it is woven so out of the yarn of desire. Its characteristic is to flutter and flit, hither and thither, through the outlets of the senses, into the external world of colour, sound, taste, smell and touch. But it can be tamed and put to good use by man. If we keep it engaged in good pursuits and good adventures, particularly in the contemplation of the Universal, the Absolute, the Eternal, that is to say, of God, then, it will not go astray and land man in ruin; for, God is the source of undying strength, of lasting joy and the deepest wisdom.

The age span, 16-30 years, is crucial, for that is the period when life adds sweetness to itself, when talents, skills, and attitudes are accumulated, sublimated and sanctified. If the tonic of unselfish *Seva* (service) is administered to the mind during this period, life's mission is fulfilled---for the process of sublimation and sanctification will be hastened by this tonic. Do not serve for the sake of reward, attracting attention, or earning gratitude, or from a sense of pride at your own superiority in skill, wealth, status or authority. Serve because you are urged by love. When you succeed, ascribe the success to the Grace of God, who urged you on, as Love within you. When you fail, ascribe the failure to your own inadequacy, insincerity or ignorance. Examine the springs of action, disinfect them from all trace of ego. Do not throw the blame on the recipients of the *seva*, or on your collaborators and co-workers, or on God.

God allows you to claim that you have served

Do not revel in the conceit that you are members of the *Seva Dhal* (service corps)---an opportunity by which thousands in this City can well profit. Egoism of that nature can undermine your efficiency as a *Dhal* member; it will certainly undermine your spiritual progress. The sense of 'I' and 'Mine' grows out of the ignorance of the majesty of God and His immanence. Anger and greed are the progeny of this evil. This malignant quartete is the root of all the calamities that man encounters upon earth.

Seva in all its forms, all the world over, is primarily *saadhana*---spiritual discipline, mental clean up. Without the inspiration given by that attitude, the urge is bound to ebb and grow dry; or, it may meander into pride and pomp. Just think for a moment: Are you serving God? Or, is God serving you? When a pilgrim stands waist deep in the Ganga, takes in his palms the sacred water and, reciting an invocatory formula, pours the water as an offering to the Deity, or *Arpan* as he calls it, what he has done is only poured Ganga into Ganga!

When you offer milk to a hungry child, or a blanket to a shivering brother on the pavement, you are but placing a gift of God into the hands of another gift to God! You are reposing the gift of God in a repository of the Divine

Principle! God serves; He allows you to claim that you have served! Without His Will, not a single blade of grass can quiver in the breeze Fill every moment with gratitude to the Giver and the Recipient of all gifts.

Nurture the will to 'give,' to renounce the little for the 'big,' the momentary for the sake of the momentous? The *Seva Dhal* Badge is not a decoration, which can be secured without a 'price.' It is a symbol of high character, generous feelings and steady endeavour. It is the external indicator of internal enthusiasm and strength, skill and faith. As iron is drawn by the magnet, these qualities that shine through you, will draw the dejected, the downcast and the distressed towards you. If you are proud and self-centred, blind to the kinship that binds all in fraternal love, the badge is a betrayal.

Progress and peace depend upon sacrifice

Eating is followed by elimination; inhalation has to be followed by exhalation; blood has to flow in and flow through, to circulate and maintain health. Taking in has to be succeeded by giving up; they are the obverse and reverse of the same process. This is true of individuals, societies, nations and the human race. Progress and peace depend upon sacrifice, renunciation and 'service.'

Do not circumscribe your *seva* to the time when I am in Bombay, or to the limits of the Dharmakshethra. Be alert to the call, everywhere, at all times; be ready with the smile, the kind word, the useful suggestion, the knowledgeful care, the pleasant reply. Look about for chances to relive, rescue or resuscitate. Train yourselves that you may render help quickly and well. *Seva* is the most rewarding form of austerity, the most satisfying and the most pleasurable! It springs out of Love and it scatters Love in profusion. It plants a seed on stone and is delighted to see it sprout!

Plant it with Love, and the seed will discover Love inside
the stone and draw sustenance therefrom.

Japa and dhyaana will render you more efficient

Dr.Mistry has mentioned in his Report that you are
doing good work in Bombay, donating blood, visiting hospital
wards, maintaining First Aid Centres in your blocks, leading
Bhajans (group singing the glory of God), promoting *Baala
Vihaars*, etc. But, it is not the quantity that matters; nor is
it the variety. It is the inner joy, the Love that you radiate
that is important. Mere sentiment and sympathy are of no
use; they must be regulated by intelligence. Shower cheer
on the sad; soothe those that have lost the way; close your
eye to the faults of others, but keep them open to discover
your own. All these are hard jobs. Practice alone can make
you perfect---practice, not only in the item of service, but,
in meditation on the Divine. *Japa* (inner muttering of holy
words) and *dhyaana* (meditation) will render you more
and more efficient in the field of service.

Dhyaana is necessary, since it leads to *Dhaarana*
(fixing the mind steadily on some desirable objective) and
Samaadhi (perfect equanimity). Practise *Dhaarana*, fixing
your gaze at night, when you sleep on the terrace in the
open, on a star that shines above your head! The practise
of *seva* will cleanse the mind and sharpen concentration.
Many members of the *Seva Dhal* have told me that they
are now able to do *Dhyaana* longer and steadier. There are
some who recommended drugs, soothers, and the like, to
those eager to do *Dhyaana;* but, they do not know that drugs
are deceptive, debilitating and dangerous, they have
deleterious consequences. I recommend *seva*.

You may be full of the urge to serve, but without
vigilance and intelligence, service cannot be fruitful.
Each little detail has to be attended to. For example, you

compel some people to sit down, instead of standing and obstructing the view for others; you do not realise that there are some who are unable to squat on the floor as a result of physical handicaps! You move more at the back and on the sides of the gatherings, leaving the central mass unattended. You need not fuss around Me; attend rather to the needs of the old, the sick, the children, those in the sun, the thirsty, the exhausted. Do not hurt the feelings of any one, by harsh treatment. Do not hinder any one's chance of *Darshan* (auidance of Baaba). Show each one the courtesy you extend to the guests you receive at your own homes. This is your home and they are your guests. Let them have sweet memories of their visit to Dharmakshethra and of the *Seva Dhal*.

This is an *adhyaathmik* army---a spiritual platoon--- engaged in cleansing itself. This movement must spread fast in India and march soon into overseas lands. Members of the *Dhal* can be sent to other places in order to train others in this practical *Vedhaantha* (philoso-phical essence of the *Vedhas*). For, if a person is imbued with the urge to serve and the belief that all are embodiments of the Divine Principle, that is itself the most potent *Japa*, the most beneficent *Dhyaana*.

Practise what you preach; be what you profess to be. Your word and your work have to tally. Keep your senses and the mind, under rigorous control; be sweet and soft in speech, do not injure the feelings of even a little child. Then, this Dharmakshethra will become a Prashaanthi Nilayam, the Abode of Peace and Joy. If the *Seva Dhal* and the volunteers of Bombay City, men and women train themselves on these lines, and succeed in this *saadhana*, one of the Festivals now celebrated at Prashaanthi Nilayam can well be held here! We can tell people that they got this grand chance as a result of the goodness, virtue and efficiency of the *Seva Dhal*.

Dharmakshethra, Bombay 19.5.1969

11. *The five hoods*

THE word, *Vishnu*, means 'That which pervades everywhere,' the Omnipresent. When people are told about an idol of Vishnu, they laugh and condemn it as foolish. But, when we desire to drink the ambrosia that the all-pervading Vishnu is, we require a spoon, a cup or a vessel. The idol is only such a contrivance, by which it is possible to consume the bliss. The cup can be of any shape or design; the joy consists in the nectar that it is able to convey to the person who is thirsty and anguished. *Raso vai sah*---God is ambrosia, sweet, sustaining, strength-giving. You can imbibe Him through a cup shaped as Nataraaja or Durga or Krishna, or Linga, or Ganesha, or Christ or any other Form that will arouse the ardour and satisfy the agony.

This is a temple, where I have installed, twenty- one year s ago, one such Form, which many yearning persons love to picture as their most favourite cup! This is the Sai Form, which sat and taught, at *Dhwaarakaamaayi*, at Shirdhi. It has a *Sesha* (serpent) with five hoods coiled behind it, the idol being in the shadow of the spread hoods.

Now, what does that represent? The five hoods are symbolic of the five senses, which have sinister poisonous potentialities. The eyes draw you away into the realm of fleshy charm and sensual beauty; the ears crave for salacious songs; the tongue overloads your digestive system with highly flavoured food; the nose leads you into jungles and laboratories in search of fragrances and scents; the sense of touch seeks softness in silk and velvet, and flounders man in mire. When man is able to master the senses, and direct them along more beneficent channels—the eye seeing God's footprints in stars and rose-petals, the ear hearing God's voice in the throats of birds and peals of thunder, the tongue tasting God's sweetness in all that appeals to it, the nose discovering fragrance in everything that recalls the glory of God, the sense of touch content to clasp the hand of the forlorn and the distressed as the beloved children of God—then, he can visualise the God installed in the cavity of the heart; that is the lesson the five-hooded *Sesha* imparts!

Be fixed in your own determination

These are days of strikes and *bandhs*. Groups of persons stop work, start shouting, or desist from activity, in order to gain some end, causing loss or dislocation to others. I would advise you all to declare a strike against the mind! Do not obey its vacillations and temptations. Be fixed in your own determination, to pursue only what your discrimination advises you as beneficent. Ignore the mind; respect the intelligence. Make the senses the servants of the intelligence, not the overlords of the mind. Tell them that the mind is dethroned, it is non-existent! Sensuousness is a disease. It denies you ease and peace. The *roga* (disease) can be cured by *Yoga*, not by *bhoga* (material enjoyment). *Bhoga* means catering to the whims and wildness of the senses; *Yoga* means the regulation and reform of the impulses of the mind which run after goals laid down by the senses! If the water is saltish, how can adding sugar make i t mo re potabl e? There are other ways to make hard and brackish water, harmless and tasty.

God is all-pervading; but, yet, we have some scientists who assert, "We have searched all outer space, we have looked for Him on the Moon; no; He is nowhere to be found. He does not exist." They do not know what to seek and where; still, they have the impudence to assert that it is not found. Is God an occupant of an identifiable body or Form, has He a habitation and a habiliment that is traditionally His? God is all this and more, He is in all this and beyond. He is the inner motivator of the very scientist who 'denies' Him! Man himself is God; all matter, even in the Moon, is suffused with the Divine Presence.

Remove the desires that surge in your heart

To search for God with the instruments of the laboratory is like trying to cure pain in the stomach by pouring drops into the eye! There is a technique and a special instrument for that purpose, which the pastmasters in that science have developed and spoken about. Equip yourselves with a clear eye, through detachment and love, sharpen your sense of discrimination, *Viveka*, so that it has no prejudice or predilection, then, you can see God in you, around you, in all that you know and feel and are. The doctor asks you to remove your shirt, before he applies the stethoscope and tries to diagnose your illness. You have another shirt covering your chest, the desires that surge in your heart! Remove that shirt, so that your real nature, that is Divinity, can be revealed to you and all who seek to know you.

All men are caskets, containing Divine Glory. But you love some of them as friendly, hate some others as unfriendly, and divide them into camps and companies. When a man is good to you, attribute that goodness to the godliness in him; when a man is bad to you, be happy that you have given him some satisfaction, by becoming the target for his attention! If he harms the body, sages are unaffected, because they know that they are not the body! If they try to harm the soul, sages know that it is impossible, for the soul is ever in Bliss!

By means of *saadhana*, become that type of sage, unaffected by pleasure and pain, loss or gain, victory or defeat. Be a witness, a disinterested witness of all the gyrations of fortune. *Vichaara* (inquiry), will reveal to you that they are fleeting fantasies of your mind, and not real. By means of *Japa* and *Dhyaana*, you can attain that identity with the Reality, which will convince you of the unreality of all except *Brahmam* (the Universal Absolute).

Guindy (Madras), 22-6-1969

Gain internal peace, internal joy; that can be done only when you act without an eye on the gain. The act must be its own reward; or rather, the act must be according to the prompting of the God within, so that its consequence is left to Him. Practise this attitude consistently and you will find great Peace welling within you and around you.

Sathya Sai Baaba

12. Mirror and comb

PREVIOUS to each Festival that is celebrated at Prashaanthi Nilayam, it has become necessary to select and authorise certain individuals for service as volunteers, or *Swayamsevaks*. The prime purpose is to provide them with a chance to train themselves in the attitudes of humility, readiness and reverence, that are so essential for one's own happiness and for social security. I have been addressing the persons selected every time, so that they may know what is expected of them, especially as the urge behind their service activities.

Among the nine steps of devotional progress, the fourth and the fifth highlight the attitude of *seva*; it is referred to as *Paadhasevanam* and *Dhaasyam* (serving the Feet of the Lord; acts offered at the Feet of the Lord; feeling oneself as the servant of the Lord). Service is basically activity arising out of the yearning to win the Grace of God. Through *seva* alone can man attain Mastery, and through mastery of the senses, the passions and the predilections, man can attain Divinity itself.

Heads bloat only through ignorance; if the Truth be known, all men will become as humble as Bharthrhari. He was a mighty emperor, who ruled from sea to sea; his decree was unquestioned; his will prevailed over vast multitudes of men. Yet, when he realised in a flash that life is but a short sojourn here below, he renounced his wealth and power, and assumed the ochre robes of the wandering monk. His countries and vassal princes shed genuine tears, for they loved and adored him. They lamented that he had donned the tattered robe of the penniless penitent, and lived on alms. "What a precious possession you have thrown away? And, what a sad bargain you have made?," they wailed. But, Bharthrhari replied, "Friends, I have made a very profitable bargain. This robe is so precious that even my empire is poor payment in exchange." That is the measure of the grandeur of the spiritual path that leads to God.

God yields Grace when His commands are followed

The spirit of sacrifice is the basic equipment of the *sevak*. Without the inspiration of the sense of sacrifice, your *seva* will be hypocrisy, a hollow ritual. Inscribe this on your heart. Inscribe it deep and clear. There are four modes of writing, dependent on the material on which the text is inscribed. The first is, writing on water; it is washed out even while the finger moves. The next is, writing on sand. It is legible, until the wind blows it into mere flatness. The third is, the inscription on rocks; it lasts for centuries, but, it too is corroded by the claws of Time. The inscription on steel can withstand the wasting touch of Time. Have this so inscribed on your heart----the axiom that "serving others is meritorious, that harming others or remaining unaffected and idle while others suffer, is sin." I am not giving you any badge to wear this time, for a badge on the shirt is a distinction you must win and not decoration to be paraded.

God is Love and can be won only through the cultivation and exercise of Love. He cannot be trapped by any trick; He yields Grace only when His commands are followed---commands to love all, to serve all. When you love all and serve all, you are serving yourself most, yourself whom you love most! For God's Grace envelops you then, and you are strengthened beyond all previous experience. If I pin the badge on your apparel, you will un-pin it soon; when it is taken off the shirt, you will feel relieved that you have been released from the obligation to love and serve. You will only play a temporary role in a drama, donning the badge and doffing it.

Bend the body, mend the senses, end the mind

In this village, there was a young man once, who acted the role of an Emperor in a folk-drama enacted on a sacred day, in the temple. The curtain went down with sunrise, but, he would not remove the crown from his head; he insisted that he was Emperor still. He continued to order his subjects about, for months. He ordered his kinsmen to execute this fellow one day, and that fellow the next day, and died himself of high fever, pretty soon! That was insanity. But, there is a sane way of behaviour, of the right role.

Wear the invisible badge of a volunteer of God at all hours and in all places. Let all the days of living be a continuous offering of Love, as an oil lamp exhausts itself in illumining the surroundings. Bend the body, mend the senses, and end the mind---that is the process of attaining the status of 'the children of immortality,' which the *Upanishadhs* have reserved for man.

God is the embodiment of sweetness. Attain Him by offering Him, who resides in all, the sweetness that

He has dowered on you. Crush the cane in the mill of *seva*, boil it in the cauldron of penitence; decolorise it of all sensual itch; offer the crystallised sugar of compassionate Love to Him.

Man is the noblest of all animals, the final product of untold ages of progressive evolution; but, he is not consciously striving to live up to his heritage. The beasts held a World Conference to confabulate on the authenticity of man's claim to be the acme of creation and the monarch of all that walks the earth. The Lion presided over the deliberations.

Man is a standing disgrace to animals

The tiger questioned the claims of man; the leopard seconded the resolution of emphatic protest. It made a devastating speech, condemning man. "He is a standing disgrace to animals everywhere. He manufactures and drinks merrily fatal poisons and is proud of his utter foolishness. He cheats his own kind and spends all his energies and resources in devising diabolical weapons to wipe out his sisters and brothers; he prods horses and dogs to run in desperate haste and gambles his earnings away, while they gallop along the track; he is cruel, greedy, immoral, insatiable and unashamed. He sets a bad example to the animal world. Though endowed with superior emotions and intelligence, his behaviour is disgusting and demeaning," he said. "We do not know if and where we will get our next meal; we have no sure place of rest. We have nothing to wrap round ourselves, except the skin. But, yet, the least of us is a far worthier child of God than this monster called man," he concluded.

The fox rose and added, "We have a season when we mate, but man, I am ashamed to say, has broken all restraints and cares for no rules. He is a law unto himself and a disaster to the rest."

The Lion rose, to sum up the arguments. He agreed with the general trend of the tirade against man, provoked by his undeserved claim to supremacy. But he refused to tar all with the same brush. He distinguished between men who are bestial and worse, and men who have transcended their bestial past, by the proper use of the special gifts of discrimination and detachment. The latter, he said, ought to be revered by all beasts as Masters, while the former deserved severe reprisals and condemnation.

Be concerned about the dust of envy and hate

Each of you has struggled upwards from the stone to plant, from plant to animal, from animal to man! Do not slide back into the beast; rise higher to Divinity, shining with the new effulgence of Love. The Divine is the energy that animates, the urge that circulates the blood in your veins, that transmits knowledge and experience through the nerves, that correlates and collects for storage the impressions your senses gather, the conclusions your intelligence garners! Keep in line with the Divine, by means of Love, Truth and Goodness.

Nowadays, there is an inevitable pair of accessories in the vanity bags of ladies and even in the pockets of gents: a mirror and a comb. You dread that your charm is endangered when your hair is in slight disarray, or when your face reveals patches of powder; so, you try to correct the impression immediately. While so concerned about this fast-deteriorating personal charm, how much more concerned should you really be about the dust of envy and hate, the patches of conceit and malice that desecrate your mind and hearts? Have a mirror and a comb for this purpose, too! Have the mirror of *Bhakthi* (devotion), to judge whether they are clean and bright and winsome; have the comb of *Jnaana* (for, wisdom, earned by discrimination straightens problems, resolves knots, and smoothes the tangle) to control and channelise the feelings and emotions that are scattered wildly in all directions.

Whatever you do, wherever you are, remember that I am with you, in you; that will save you from conceit and error. That will make your *seva* worthy of the people you serve.

Prashaanthi Nilayam, 26-6-1969

*Little children are trained to walk, by means of a three- wheeled contraption which they hold and push along. The **Pranava** is such a contraption, with the three wheels of **A U** and **M**, the **Omkaara** Tricycle. Holding it, man can learn to use the two feet of **bhakthi** and **vairaagya**. If he gives up his hold on the **Omkaara**, he plumps down on the ground helplessly. If he walks on with the help of the **Pranava** japa, he can certainly realise the glory of the **Brahmam**, which is the very substance of the Universe.*

Sathya Sai Baaba

13. House and home

Y OUR Vice-Chancellor Gokak spoke in very charming Kannada, as is his wont, since he is a poet and writer in that language. I too shall speak in that language, though I usually speak only in Thelugu at such gatherings; pay attention to the matter, rather than the style, for, I speak to you of spiritual disciplines which will grant you lasting benefit.

Bhaaratheeya Samskrithi (India's Culture) has Prapanchavyaapthi (World-wide spread) since it can correct and canalise the human emotions and motives along healthy productive routes. It is sacred and basic and it can establish peace and joy in the hearts of all. It seeks to strike roots into life through the mothers, and children on their laps. Women have been its custodians and promoters; men have a secondary role. And, among women, you girl students, who will be the leaders of women in the coming days, the examples which all women wish to emulate, must understand and practise this culture, so that it may be preserved and it may flourish. The keenness to acquire education is now very evident among the daughters of the nation and so, great hope can be placed on them, in this field of reconstruction. Education must be for life, not for a living. Women have proved throughout the centuries in Indian History that they have the courage, the vision, and the intelligence needed to dive into the depths of spiritual science and discipline. Maithreyi, Meera, Gargi, Sulabha, Choodala, Mahaadhevi, Aandal, are standing examples of the mighty heroines of the spiritual adventure into the realms of God-realisation.

Reject the riches and seek the Reality instead

Woman has been extolled in ancient scriptures as well as classical poetry as *Grihalakshmi*, the Goddess of Prosperity in the Home. She is the *Dharmapathni* (the companion in virtue of the husband) in the fulfilment of the duties and rights of wedded life as a householder. While learning home science, you may be getting trained in the art of making the home happy and full of harmony and health. You have to learn also how to steer clear of hatred, malice, greed, anger, anxiety, pride and other obstacles that come in the way of inner peace. It is not enough if the home budget is balanced; the wife (and the mother) must learn the art of having a balanced view of life, which will not be affected by triumphs and troubles, gains or losses, victory or defeat. This balance can be got only by reliance on God, faith in the in- dwelling God. Thyaagaraaja sang of the dilemma that faces every one, when confronted with riches on the one hand and the Inner Reality of God on the other. Thyaagaraaja rejected riches and sought the Reality, instead.

One discipline you must heed, namely, the control of the senses; if you give them free rein, they will drag

you into calamity. Education must render you monarch of
your talents, your tools for acquiring knowledge. The eye,
the ear, the tongue are like wild horses that have no bit
between the teeth; learn the art of *dhyaana* by which the
senses can be controlled and the will directed inwards,
towards the mastery of feelings and emotions. A nation that
has no bridle on its sensuality can never thrive or survive.

You are mastering what is called 'Home Science'; but,
what is a home? How is it different from a house? The home
is filled with love, with the sacrifice that love involves, the
joy that love radiates, and the peace that love imparts. The
brick and mortar structure where parents and children
spend their lives is not a home; children do not yearn for
it, parents do not find peace therein!

Make the shrine room the centre of your home

Many educated women have converted the home into a
hotel, what with the cook, the *maali* (the gardener), the
servants, the *aayah* (nursery maid), the bearer, the chauffeur
who clutter the whole place! She is just a scintillating doll,
darting in and through the rooms; she is often a millstone
round the neck of the husband, whom she leads about and
lords over, to his utter discomfiture. She engages herself in
spending money, shopping for things of her wayward fancy,
in order to keep up social appearances; she idles away the time
in lazy lounging and medicating herself for imaginary illness.
She becomes a burden on her spouse and children.

The centre of every home must be the shrine room; the
fragrance of flower and incense emanating from there must
pervade the home and purify it. The mother must set the
example in making the shrine the heart of the household.
She must enforce discipline over the children in personal
cleanliness, in humility and hospitality, in good
manners and acts of service. She must persuade the

children by example and precept to revere elders and to allot some time both in the morning and evening for prayer, and for silent meditation.

The shrine room has to be kept clean and consecrated; special festival days marked out in each religion, should be observed, so that the significance will impress the young minds. However self- centred and haughty the husband is, by systematic regulation of the domestic time-table, with worship of God as its focal point, the man can be made to realise how a God-centred Home is home of peace and joy. He too will soon fall in and be a pillar of faith.

Learn the effect of different types of food on character

The mother herself should look after the children during the early years; if the child is handed over to servants and *aayahs*, it will learn their habits of living and speech and will weep only when they die, not when the mother dies! For, the child starts loving the *aayah* more than the mother, who has shoved them on to another as a nuisance and a bother! The mother must herself prepare food for the home; for, food that is prepared with love and served with a smile is much more sustaining and strengthening than food cooked by a hired woman and served by a disgruntled refractory kitchen boy!

I am glad cookery and nutrition are included in your syllabus; I smell even here, while on the dias, some dishes being got ready in your culinary laboratory! Your knowledge of cookery reaches far, I must admit! The constituents of a tasty dish attract the senses and titillate them, no doubt. But, I hope you learn also about the distinction between the *Saathwik* (calmness promoting), the *Raajasik* (emotion producing) and the *Thaamasik* (sloth encouraging) types of food and of the effect of these on char-

acter. The mind is the key to health and happiness and
so, food must be so chosen that it does not affect the
mind adversely; along with *Saathwik* food, the mind
must also be given special diet like *Dhyaana, Japa,
Naamasmarana*, etc. to keep it sound and steady.

Home is the temple where the family is nurtured

The status of the mother in the home is one of
authority; now, even colleges like this, try to train up only
the Wife, not the Mother. The Home for which science
caters here is the home where the wife rules, not where
the mother spreads her affection and shapes the future of
the country and its culture! Let the children, even
grown-up boys and girls, touch the feet of the father and
mother every morning, before the daily tasks are started;
it will generate a reverential atmosphere in the home. Five
minutes in the shrine room and the *namaskaaram*
(prostration) for parents---let this be the daily routine. The
Upanishadhs recommend this as the basic requirements
of our culture. *Maathru dhevo bhava; Pithru dhevo bhava;
Aacharya dhevo bhava!*

The home is the temple where the family, each
member of which is a moving temple, is nurtured and
nourished. The mother is the high priest of this House of
God. Humility is the incense with which the house is filled.
Reverence is the lamp that is lit, with love as the oil and
faith as the wick. Spend the years of your lives, dedicating
them for such worship, in the homes that you will found.
I bless you that through your faith and strength, devotion
and dedication may increase in this land.

College of Home Science, Bangalore, 26-7-1969

14. *The voice of the ocean*

THE seeker has to be very vigilant about his point of view, the things he seeks to visualise, the things he longs to cast his eyes on. For, it is *dhrishti* (the view) that decides attachment, sorrow, passion, etc. You are the noblest being yet created, and so, you have to develop a sight that sees no high or low, that sees all as suffused with divinity, and therefore, not different one from another. Shankara declared, "Make your *dhrishti* charged with *jnaana*; then, the seen will appear in its true light as *Brahman*."

Such sight is called divine, supernatural, super-sensual and auspicious. Each body that you see before you is a mirror in which if only you open your eyes you can see the image of God. The God in you is in each of them, too. Do not imagine the others to be distinct, they are only you, in so many mirrors. The world is filled with your kith and kin; all are sparks from the same flame. The Geetha says, "*Pandiths* (the learned) see *Brahman* in the scholar, the sage, the venerable and the venerator, the

cow, the elephant, the dog and the eater of canine flesh."
Such *Pandiths* are very rare on the face of the earth;
men claim to be *Pandiths* on the basis of the scholarship
they parade, not the vision they have won.

Some *Pandiths* explain the Geetha verse, which declares
that God incarnates when *Dharma* (virtue) declines, in this
way: "*Dharma* stood on four legs in the *Kritha* (golden or fulfilled) Age; it had only three in the next age, the *Thretha*;
(three legged) later, in the *Dhwaapara* (twin based) Age, it
stood precariously on two and now in the *Kali* (iron or harsh)
Age, it has only one leg to stand on!" They say also in the same
breath, that God incarnated as Raama in the *Thretha* Age,
and as Krishna in the *Dhwaapara* Age, with the avowed purpose of restoring *Dharma*! According to them, when Krishna
incar-nated *Dharma* had two legs, but, when His human
career was closed, *Dharma* lost one more leg and had to survive
in agony, having only one solitary leg! Can such absurdity be
ever believed? No. The Incarnations of God have always fulfilled their tasks. *Dharma* has always been restored, in full.

Truth is the lamp that dispels darkness

What they re-established on firm foundations is
Sathya (Truth). For, as the *Vedhas* (sacred scriptures)
announce, there is no *Dharma* higher than Truth. Truth
gets hidden, appears distorted, is declared as failing; so, the
Avathaar (divine incarnation) asserts its validity and value,
once again. God wears Truth; the good seek Truth; the bad
are rescued by Truth. Truth liberates; Truth is power;
Truth is freedom. It is the lamp that illumines the heart
and dispels doubt and darkness. The effulgence of God
is Truth. Welcome God in your heart. Install Him there
as a result of Yearning. Be always concerned with
Brahman; then, you are entitled to be known as a
Brahmin; if you are concerned with the skin and all that

it contains, that entitles you only to be known as a *Chandaala*, who works on leather and skin!

There was Kanaka, born in a low caste. He was an ardent devotee, yearning in unbearable anguish to see Krishna. So, he went to Udipi, where there is a famous Krishna Temple, established by the great sage, Madhwaachaarya himself. Being of low birth, he could not enter the temple and see the charming idol of Krishna. He stood before the outer door, but the idol was hidden by the Flag- post in front of the shrine. He went round the outer wall and sought some crevice amidst the stones through which he could earn a faint glimpse. He saw a stone was loose: with his fingers, he scooped out the mortar and he made a narrow chink, and when he looked eagerly through it, he saw only the back of the idol. But he was overcome with delight! He danced in ecstasy, singing the glory of Krishna. Just at the moment, the idol turned towards him and Krishna granted him the full vision of His Charm and majesty. Yearning was rewarded with Grace. Yearning leads to surrender, and surrender gives the highest joy. Leave everything to His Will, accept whatever happens, whether pleasant or painful.

Have firm faith in God and His Compassion

There was once a rich merchant in Baghdad, who was leading a virtuous God-fearing life. He had a daughter whom he adored greatly, for she was the very embodiment of virtue. The father decided that he would give her in marriage only to a young man who was intimately devoted to God, regardless of any other excellence or handicap. He searched for such a groom in caravanserais, mosques and places where holy persons were likely to gather. One Friday, he noticed in the mosque a fair young man, on his knees, even after all else had left, crying out to God most

endearingly and with great sincerity. He approached him
and asked whether he would marry his daughter. He said:
"I am the poorest of the poor; I have a leaky roof over my
head, and a gravel floor whereon I sit. Who will wed such
a beggar? I shall marry if some one who would not object
to my spiritual *saadhana*, consents to share my poverty."

The merchant felt that he was the most eligible
groom and the wedding was celebrated soon. His
daughter came to the *fakir's* (merdicant's) residence and
started cleaning the floor. She was happy that her
husband was of her own heart; she too was pilgrim on
the road to God, a practioner of spiritual exercises. While
sweeping the floor, she found in a corner a plate with a
piece of bread on it. She asked her husband why it was
kept there, and he replied: "I kept it by, lest tomorrow
when I go on my rounds, we may not get enough to eat."
At this, the wife replied, "I am ashamed of you. You have
so little faith in Allah. He who gives us hunger, will He not
give us bread too? I shall not live with a person of this
nature. You have no faith in God and His Compassion."
After saying this she left the *fakir* to himself.

Live without being inimical to any being

The Geetha says that if you give up all *Dharma* and
take refuge in Him alone, then He will save you from sin
and wipe your tears. Giving up *Dharma* does not mean that
you can bid farewell to virtue and righteous action; it
means, you have to give up the egoism that you are the
'doer,' be confirmed in the faith that He is the 'doer' of every
deed. That is the genuine 'giving up.' There are in the world
Bhojanaalayas (hotels), *Vaidhyaalayas* (Hospitals),
Vilaasaalayas (Homes of Entertainment, Theatres),
Vihaaraalayas (Places of sport, gymkhaanas), *Vichith-
raalayas* (Museums, Palaces of Art, etc.), etc. But, however

they are named, they are all *Duhkhaalayas* (Homes of Sorrow). The only *Aanandhanilaya* (Home of Joy) is the *Dhevaalaya* (Temple of God), that is to say, one's own body where God is the inner Guide and Guardian.

On this *Guru Poornima* Day, the counsel that I can give you is this: Do not hate anyone, follow the Geetha prescription to spiritual health, *Adhweshtaa Sarva bhoothaanaam*, 'without being inimical to any being.' The reason for this injunction is that God is the inner *Aathma* in everything that exists. So, injury inflicted on any being is sacrilege, self-injury. Love is transformed into poison if hate contaminates it. Love some, but do not hate the rest, for that hate will foul the love and make it mortal. Love comes automatically to the realised soul; but, the spiritual aspirant has to cultivate it by means of service and inquiry into the unity of the *Aathman*. Love must flow not from the tongue, or from the head only, but chiefly from the heart.

Poor progress in *Saadhana* is as bad as failure

You get the marks that your answers at the examination deserve, not more, not less. Sometimes, if you secure only 5 or 6 out of a total of 100, even the 5 or 6 may be cancelled and you will be assigned just a zero. For, there is not much to choose between zero and the 5 or 6 you were able to collect. But, if you get a number very near the minimum needed for a pass, the 2 or 3 that you fall short of will be added on as grace marks and you are very likely to be promoted. This is true of *saadhana* also. Poor progress in it is as bad as failure, whereas good progress will be appreciated and Grace will pull you through.

On the *Guru Poornima* Day, people generally take initiation into spiritual life from some Preceptor or get directions for some vow or fast or vigil. These preceptors cannot claim the status of the *Guru* as delineated in the *sloka, Guru Brahma, Guru Vishnu, Guru Dhevo Maheswarah; Guru saakshaath Parabrahma,* etc. The *Guru* extolled therein is the sage who has transcended Name and Form and is beyond the effect of the three *gunas* or attributes; he is neither good nor bad; neither passionate nor dull; neither enthusiastic nor uninterested. He is unaffected, calm, content. He is the *Aathma,* having realised that the *Aathma* is the One and Only. He makes you cast off the fear of death and birth, he renders you fit for the vision of the eternal absolute Truth.

Only dedication will take the prayers to God

If you do not come across such preceptors, do not get downhearted; pray for guidance and from your own heart you will receive the Geetha that you need from the Charioteer who is there. You can easily get plenty of preceptors the moment you seek; for, it has now become a profession, full of competing practitioners, each one trying to collect as many disciples, as much money, and as wide a reputation as he can. There are some who have developed swollen heads, while others suffer from short sight or bitterness or itching palm. How can persons challenging each other for dry disputations be revered as *Gurus*? When they do not possess, along with the elation of scholarship, the ecstasy of Divine Experience, they are not entitled to that holy mission.

However superfine the paper, however artistic the envelope, however poetic the composition of the letter, it will not reach the addressee by post when it lacks the 20 paise stamp! So too, the trappings, vestures, shawls, robes, and rosaries are ineffective; they cannot reach the addressee, God. What will take their prayers to the addressee is the 20 paise stamp---dedication or *Bhakthi.*

He who seeks a *Guru* can find him in every word spoken within his hearing, in every incident that happens around him. The Deity, *Dakshinaamurthi* (primal divine teacher of eternal spiritual wisdom) was walking along a wide seashore alone, immersed in deep meditation. He turned towards the waves and watched the unending succession of breakers. He saw a dry little twig on the crest of a wave in the distance; it was being passed on from one wave to another, from trough to crest, from crest to trough, until it was cast on the sands on the shore, near where He stood! Dakshinaamurthi was astounded at the egoism of the Ocean that would not give asylum to even a tiny twig. Sensing His reaction, the Ocean declared, in words that He could understand, "Mine is neither egoism nor anger; it is only the duty of self- preservation. I should not allow the slightes t blot to deface my grandeur. If I allow this twig to mar my splendour, it will be the first step in my downfall." Then, Dakshinaamurthi smiled within Himself, admiring the vigilance of the mighty Ocean. He pictured the incident as a great lesson in spiritual endeavour. The slightest twig of desire, if it falls on the mind, has to be immediately lifted out of the pure waters and thrown off. That was the lesson to be learnt.

Three stages in the journey to reach God

The *Raamaayana* teaches that Seetha had to suffer separation from Raama as a result of a tiny little desire: to own the golden-hued deer! If only she had cast it off her mind, as the Ocean did! Be free from the bondage of desire---this is the refrain in the *Raamaayana*, the *Mahaabhaaratha*, the *Bhaagavatha*, the Bible, the Quoran, and all the scriptures of mankind.

Each religion exhorts those who are attracted by it to meditate on God in certain Form known by a certain Name; but, one who is aware that He is all Names and all Forms will adopt a sound which is profoundly significant, which summarises all Names, namely, the *Pranava* (*OM*) sound, the *Akshara* (Unchanging, indestructible). Through the changing to the unchanging, that is the journey. From the *kshara* to the *Akshara*. There are three steps or stages in this journey. "I am YOURS"; "YOU are Mine!" and, finally, "I am YOU!" Every *saadhaka* has to walk from one to the other, and reach the journey's end. Move on, don't halt.

It is good to be born in a church, but it is not good to die in it. Grow and rescue yourselves from the limits and regulations, the doctrines that fence your freedom of thought, the ceremonials and rites that restrict and re-direct. Reach the point where churches do not matter, where all roads end, from where all roads run.

There is no shortcut to attain Self-realisation

Duth from Calcutta said that it is a pretty hard assignment to listen closely, reflect deeply, and practise faithfully, the three stages prescribed in the *Shaasthras*. Of course, it is. Attaining Self-realisation is not done by a trick, or a ruse; it has no short cut. Listen to what happened to sage Raamadhaas of Bhadhraachalam, the singer who was imprisoned by the Nawab of Golconda, for misappropriation of public funds (to renovate the Raama Temple at Bhadhraachalam), whose liberation from jail was effected by Raama and Lakshmana themselves paying the Nawab the sum appropriated!

Raamadhaas had piled up a large mass of palmyra leaves, on each of which he had written with his style a song on Raama. When his eyes fell on the heap one day, a thought struck him: Did I compose these songs for my pleasure? Or, for pleasing Raama?" He wanted to know those songs which had pleased Raama, and fling away those which did not. He decided to throw the whole bundle into the Godhaavari River and let Raama save those which He approved. Almost the whole lot sank in the depths; only 108 floated and were recovered. They alone had arisen from the heart; the rest smacked of cleverness, artificiality, panditry, pedantry. Prayers must emanate from the heart, where God resides, and not from the head, where doctrines and doubts clash.

Faith in God being within the heart, faith in His constant presence and constant guidance---these will confer courage, virtue, and illumination. The *Shaasthras* say, have faith in the doctor, so that you may get cured of illness; have faith in the *manthra* (holy formula) with which the preceptor initiates you, for then alone can your *saadhana* be fruitful; have faith in the sacredness of the temple, for then alone is your pilgrimage profitable; have faith in the astrologer's predictions, for, without it, why bother yourselves with him and his abracadabra? Have faith in the *Guru*, for then alone will your steps be steady and firm, on the path to Self-realisation. Faith in the *Guru* should bring faith in the *Aathma* (free Self), or else, the *Guru* is a handicap.

Guru Poornima, Prashaanthi Nilayam, 29-7-1969

When worship is rendered with a view to fulfil desires and realise wishes, the precious prize will be lost. Worship must cleanse the heart, so that the indwelling God may shine in all His Glory; but desires tarnish, instead of cleansing.

Sathya Sai Baaba

15. The Achaarya....as God

THIS day, *Guru Pournami*, is celebrated by people as
thanksgiving Day for their spiritual preceptors, those
who initiated them into spiritual disciplines, *manthra*
recitals, meditation, *japa* and the study of sacred texts.
We have a popular saying, "Without a preceptor, all
learning is blind." But, this refers to authentic *Gurus*,
those who have the double qualification of *gu* and *ru*: *gu*
meaning, devoid of *gunas* and *ru* meaning, devoid of
ruupa---that is to say, those who have transcended Form
and Flavour, those who have merged in God, or the *Aathma*
Itself. It is only these who can help you to attain.

The *Vedhas* declare that the Mother, the Father, the
Achaarya (Preceptor) have to be treated as God. The
Mother brings forth and trains the emotions and
intelligence, and fosters and feeds the body during the
critical first few years of life. The father protects and guides,
and supports till the child is able to fend for itself. The
Achaarya opens the inner eye; he shows the way, for joy
and happiness, here and hereafter. So, the responsibility

of the *guru* is overwhelming. Today, we have *gurus* who scheme for earning riches and status; their minds are poisoned by the fumes of egotism and greed. They cause even the faithful to desert the path of discipline which they have entered. Others have vast learning and consequently, they suffer from swelled head and the infection of competition. God will not accept such men as His favourites. You may put in an envelope a letter written in exceptionally beautiful style, containing precious sentiments and decorated with charming drawings---but, unless you affix a 20 paise stamp, it cannot reach the person whom you address. On the other hand, the paper may be crumpled and cheap; the sentiments may be commonplace; the style may be poor. But, fix the stamp---it reaches the destination! What is essential is the yearning, the anguish. If that is evident, the prayer will reach God.

Eternal vigilance is the price of peace

Every object in nature, every incident in time, is really speaking, teaching you a lesson, as the postal stamp does. Dakshinaamurthy was one morning walking in slow steps along the sea-beach. He looked at the waves---and drew a lesson therefrom. He saw the waves slowly but systematically, carrying towards the shore a bit of straw, passing it on from one crest to another, until it was deposited on land! The sea is a broad expanse, it is deep and mighty. But, yet, it is constantly engaged in clearing itself from all extraneous things. It knows that, you must not neglect a desire, for the reason that it is a straw. Force it back, on to the shore, where it can do no harm. Eternal vigilance is the price of peace and happiness. Dakshinaamurthy exclaimed, "Wonderful! The Sea has taught me a great lesson."---the lesson that danger lurks, when desire raises its head.

Take the example of Seetha. She was the daughter of the greatest *jnaani* and philosopher of the age,

Janaka. She was the consort of the Lord; her father-in-law the mighty emperor Dasharatha. Nevertheless, when her lord was exiled and sent into the forest for 14 years, she gave up all the luxuries to which she had become accustomed, and insisted on being taken by Him into the same forest, as His companion. What tremendous detachment, what admirable adherence to the dictates of morality! But, when she saw in the woods, a 'golden deer', desire entered her heart; as a result she had to suffer the agony of separation from the Lord. That is the tragedy of desire, arising from the senses and the mind. He who instructs you to give up desire is the real *Guru*.

Keep the heart cool, pure, soft as the moonlight

Each religion emphasises one name and one Form of God and recommends them for acceptance. Some even insist that God has no other Name or Form. But, the Reality is beyond name and form, *Akshara* (the indestructible, eternal) as the characteristic and *Om* as the Form. You reach the *Akshara* stage---the stage of attributeless unity---in three steps of *Saadhana*: (i) I am Thine, (ii) Thou art mine, and (iii) Thou art myself. Through *Saadhana*, one must transcend the duality of I and You. I is only the reflection of You in this body. The consummation is reached when duality is superseded. That is why it has been declared, "It is good to be born in a church; but, it is not good, to die in it." That is to say, before life ends one must go beyond the limits set by institutionalised religion and reach the vast limitless expanse of the *Aathman*, which pervades all.

As the Judge from Calcutta said just now, in his speech, the head is of no help in this *Saadhana*; the heart must win the goal. Raamadhaas of Bhadhraachalam used to write on palm leaves hundreds of songs on his favourite Deity, Raama; the leaves accumulated into a gigantic pile. One day, Raamdhaas stood by its side and wondered, "Am I the fellow who wrote all this? Did I write them for my satisfaction or for pleasing Raama?" He carried the whole pile and threw them into the Godhaavari River; Only 108 songs floated above the waters; the rest sank and were lost for ever. Those 108 came forth from the heart; the rest were products of intelligence, cleverness. They rose from the head. God does not reside in the head; He is *Hridhayavaasi*, the Dweller in the Heart. Keep the heart cool, pure and soft---as the moonlight is on this day---the *Guru Poornima* Day.

For this, your mind has to be cleansed by the mind only. Just as you shape an iron sickle or axe with an iron hammer, the mind is the shaper and shaped, both. The power behind the mind which helps it to shape it well, is Faith in God. That is why it is declared that one must have faith in God, holy places, the scriptures, the *manthra*, the soothsayer, the drug and the teacher. Cultivate that Faith and everything else will be added unto you.

Prashaanthi Nilayam, 29.7.1969

Our failures and disappointments, our setbacks and our problems, need not retard our progress, if only we use the obstacles as "stepping stones" and not as "stopping stones." The man worth while, is the man who can smile, when everything goes dead wrong.

Sathya Sai Baaba

16. *Guru Poornima*

ADWESHTAA *Sarva Bhoothaanaam* (with no ill-will against living being), *Sarva Bhootha hithe rathaah* (always engaged in promoting the well being of all beings), *Samah shathrou cha mithre cha* (considering foe and friend alike)---jewels like these contained in the Geetha, are, as known to all, pointers to the need for Universal Love. The Geetha offers plenty such, to help the worldly to swim across the sea of sorrow. In the Geetha the Lord lays down the ideal, "Do all acts for Me; become Mine; be devoted to Me, giving up all other attachments."

By declaring that man shall not bear ill-will towards the entire world of living beings, the Geetha is positing a lesson with invaluable inner meaning: that in all beings and even things, there is moving and revolving, as an active illumining Principle, the Divine, appropriately called as *Aathma*. The *Vedhic* assertions, *Ishaavasyamidham Sarvam* (All this is enveloped in God), *Sarva Bhootha antharaathma* (The inner core of all Beings is He), *Vaasudhevah sarvamidham* (All this is God, Vaasudheva)—firmly establish this profound Truth.

It is a wrong against God, this Omnipresent Divine, to hate living beings, to injure them; that is to say, it is as bad as hating and injuring oneself---the reason being that the injurer is as much a living being with God as his core, as the injured. Potharaaju, the classic Thelugu Poet, had realised this truth; so he writes in the *Bhaagavatha*:

> *"Grant me, O Lord,*
> *So ready to reward rigorous self-control!*
> *Grant me, O Lord,*
> *The adoration of Thy Lotus Feet*
> *The comradeship of those who adore*
> *Thy Lotus Feet*
> *And give me compassion,*
> *Deep, vast, unlimited,*
> *Towards all beings in all the worlds.*

Love cannot be tarnished by malice or hate

Until you become aware of your own Divinity (*Devathathwa*) so long as you are conscious of your distinct individuality (*Jeeva-thath-wa*)---so long as you feel you are you and God is God, you cannot but struggle, with some attitudes and objectives. This is the stage called the *Saadhaka* stage. During that stage, you must endeavour to equip yourself with the above mentioned qualities of Love, Sympathy and Compassion. For, without these, *Yoga* and *Jnaana* cannot be secured.

Love is vital. Love is Divine. To render an act fit to be offered to God and pure enough to win His Grace, it has to be a manifestation of Love. The brighter the manifestation, the nearer you are to God. *Prema* is not affected or modified by considerations of caste or creed, or religion; it cannot be tarnished by envy, malice or hate.

Preserve Love from being poisoned by these evils; endeavour to cultivate hatred-less, distinction-free

feelings. The root of all religions, the substance of all
scriptures, the rendezvous of all roads, the inspiration of
all individuals is the Principle of *Prema* (Love) . It is the
firmest foundation for man's mission of Life. It is the Light
that ensures World Peace and World Prosperity.

Fill every word of yours with Love, fill every act of
yours with Love. The word that emerges from your tongue
shall not stab like the knife, nor wound like the arrow, nor
hit like the hammer. It has to be a foundation of sweet
nectar, a counsel of consoling *Vedhaanthic* wisdom, a soft
path of blossoms; it must shower peace and joy.

Love knows no fear, shuns falsehood

Love for Love's sake; do not manifest it for the sake of
material objects or for the fulfillment of worldly desires.
Desire begets anger, anger provokes sin, for under its
impact, friends are seen as foes. Anger is at the bottom of
every variety of calamity. Therefore do not fall a prey to it.
Treat every one---whoever he may be---with the all-inclusive
compassion of Love. This constructive sympathy has to
become the spontaneous reaction of all mankind.

Saturate the breath---while you inhale and while you
exhale---in Love. Saturate each moment in Love. Love knows
no fear. Love shuns falsehood. Fear drags man into falsehood,
injustice and wrong. Love does not crave for praise; that is its
strength. Only those who have no Love in them itch for
reward and reputation. The reward for Love is Love itself.

When you are eager to place offerings before the Lord,
instead of transitory materials, let your offering be Love.
Love is the very Light of Love; it is the only comprehensive
Code of Conduct.

Love is no merchandise; do not bargain about its cost.
Let it flow clear from the heart, as a stream of Truth, a

river of wisdom. Let it not emanate from the head, nor from the tongue. Let it emerge, full and free, from the heart. This is the highest duty, the noblest Godliness.

Start the day with Love. Live the day with Love. Fill the day with Love. Spend the day with Love. End the day with Love. This is the way to God. If you repeat 'God' 'God' but receive anger and lust, hate and envy into your heart, you cannot rise into Divinity, you will only slide into Diabolism.

Today's Festival is called *Guru Poornima*; it is a name full of meaning. *Poornima* means, the effulgent Full Moon. *Guru* means (*Gu*-ignorance; *Ru*-destroyer) he, who removes the darkness and delusion from the heart and illumines it with the Higher Wisdom.

The message and lesson of *Guru Poornima* Day

The Moon and the Mind are inter-related, as object and image. On this Day, the Moon is full, fair and cool, its light is fresh, pleasant and peaceful. So the Light of the Mind too has to be pleasing and pure. This is the Message of the Day. That is to say, in the firmament of the Heart, the Moon is the Mind. There are clouds there, thick and heavy---the sensual desires and worldly activities, which mar your joy at the Light of the Moon. Therefore, let the strong breeze of Love scatter the clouds and confer on you the cool glory of moon light. When devotion shines full, the sky in the heart becomes a bowl of beauty and life is transformed into a charming avenue of *Aanandha*. That beauty of heart, that *Aanandha* (bliss) in life can be won through the mind, if the lesson of this Day is remembered and realised.

Strengthened by Swaami's Grace, encouraged by Swaami's Blessings, engage in *Saadhana* (spiritual practice) and achieve success by realising the Goal of Life.

Prashaanthi Nilayam, 29.7.1969

17. The spider in the same web

FESTIVAL Days like this are marked out in the calendar, in order to waken the mind of man, which is apt to doze off in sloth or complaisance after some spurt of *Saadhana*. They are like alarm bells, which go off at intervals during the year, warning men of the journey ahead and the goal beyond the horizon. "*Thasmaath jaagratha jaagratha!*"--- "therefore, be warned, be warned!" say the sages. Awake, arise, stop not until the goal is attained.

Man should not yield to thirst for the world's gifts; he should yearn for the gift of Grace. That yearning will impel Krishna to visualise Himself in order to quench the agony. Bharatheeya culture has emphasised the inner meaning of the scriptures, and the deeper significances of rites and ceremonies. It revels in symbolism, but, it has always encouraged seekers to rend the veil and learn the principle enshrined in the symbol. It has advised the reciters of the sacred *Vedhas* to recite the hymns with a full awareness of the meaning of the paeans and prayers.

We are today celebrating the Advent of Krishna. The *Avathaar* (Incarnation) in the Krishna Form has vast mysteries enshrined in it. Brindhaavan (the forest of Brindha) is the tangled jungle of life. The cows tended by Lord Krishna in Brindhaavan are none other than the humans that are helpless without His care and guidance. Gokula (the herds of cows) is the name given in the *Bhaagavatham* (Story of the Glory of the Lord) to the region where Krishna tended the cows. '*Go*' means also the individual who is enclosed in the body. So, Gokula is the region inhabited by man. You know that in Thelugu, Geetha means a streak! And, in the *Upanishadhs* God is described as a "streak of lightning, flashing through a thick blue cloud;" Krishna is 'blue,' of the blue cloud; the *Vedhas* say, *neela thoyadha*; the *Bhaagavatham* says, *neela megha*. Both mean that He is as deep as the sky or the sea and so His colour is that of the sea and the sky!

Trace the Lord in your heart and hold fast

The streak mentioned in the *Vedhas* is the *geetha*, the true '*geetha* of Krishna. The Gopees, the simple sincere cowherd maids of Gokula, sought Krishna within or behind every bush and bower, for He was fascinating them, but ever keeping Himself away! This is only another way of describing the search for the God that we know to be within us, who eludes our efforts to sink into that sweetness. Krishna is hiding in the recesses of your hearts; you have to trace Him there and hold fast. He runs away, but leaves footprints marked by the split milk on which He has trodden, in His hurry to be beyond our reach. Yes, the lesson is: recognise His Footprints in every thing of beauty, every act of goodness, every tear of gratitude, every sigh of compassion, and discover Him in the bower of your own heart, filled with the fragrance of Love and Light of Virtue.

When you have to be shown the moon, they say, "Look at the tip of that branch of that tree!" As if, the

moon is right on the top of that branch! There is a long long
way to go, to reach the moon; but, you can see it from afar,
as a round disc emitting cool, comfortable light. So too, the
Bhaagavatham and other epics and poems show the Lord
and help you to see Him enough to arouse the keenness to
approach Him nearer; that is all! Each book leads you from
one stage to another, revealing more and more of the
beneficence of God, until you are filled with insatiable
yearning for Him. That yearning is its own reward; it will
transform the Will of God into the Form you long to see. A
rolling stone, it is said, gathers no moss; the stone that
stays put is encrusted with moss. The mind that rolls from
book to book, that delineates the charm of Divinity, cannot
get encrusted with the moss of material desire.

The Lord has no favourites or foes

God is not drawn into desire; He has no wants; He is
full, free and ever content. He has no aversions or
attractions. He has no bonds of kith or kin. One poet has sung,
"O Krishna! O Gopaala! I do not count on your being kind to
me, or being moved by my appeals for mercy. Don't I know that
you killed with your own hands your maternal uncle? You killed
the very nurse who came endearingly to you in order to feed
you at her breast! With no iota of compassion towards the father
of your dearest devotee, you tortured him and killed him while
the son, Prahlaadha, was looking on! You approached Bali as
if for alms, and when he gladly placed all he had at your feet,
you trampled on his head and pressed him down into the nether
regions! How can a heart that has no tenderness, melt at my
misery?" Yes! the Lord is above all attachments; he has no
favourites or foes. You decide the distance between Him and
yourselves. *Moksha* is the stage when *moha* (attachment)
attains *kshaya* (extinction). How, then, can the Grantor of
Moksha be Himself abridged by attachment?

God has no will or want. He does not confer or withhold. He is the eternal witness. To put it in the language that you can understand, He is like the postman, who is not concerned with the contents of the letters that he hands over to the addresses; one letter might communicate victory, another, defeat; you receive what you have worked for. Do good and have good in return; be bad and accept the bad that comes back to you. That is the law, and there is really no help or hindrance.

The *Raajasik* and *Saathwik Mahaathmas*

Raavana is a *Mahaathma* (great person); Thaataki, described as an ogress, is also a *mahaathma*! That is to say, they had superhuman prowess and mysterious powers. All are Divine; God is the inner motivator of everyone. They are *mahaathmas* not only in the sense that all are *mahaathmas*: They are *Raajasik Mahaathmas*, enslaved by their emotions and passions, quick to hate and slow to forget the slights inflicted on them. Raama and Lakshmana are *Saathwik Mahaathmas*, embodiments of the prowess and powers that righteousness and virtue can endow.

A red-hot iron hammer can be hammered into shape by a cold iron hammer. So too, a person red hot with emotion and passion can be hammered by the hammer that knows no heat of anger or hate. That is the reason Raama was able to defeat Raavana and destroy him. Why? The very word *Sathwa* means strength, power, vigour, vitality. For, virtue is power, good-ness is power. A person is angry because he is weak; he is a bully, because he is a coward; he utters lies, because he is sure he deserves to be punished and he is too weak to welcome it gladly!

The human baby, born as innocence in *Dharmakshethra* (in the realm of *Dharma*), in the fullness of *Sathawaguna*, gathers, as the years roll by, the moss of

Rajas and *Thamas*, and lands itself in the conflict-ridden area of Kurukshethra. That is the story of *Mahaabhaaratha* in each life. Kuruskshethra is a battlefield between *Maamakaah* (our people) and *Paandavaah* (the fair people). That is what the very first *shloka* of the Geetha announces! What does this really mean? On one side stand the *Raajasik* (passionate) and *Thaamasik* (impure) impulses fed by the sense of mine and our; on the other side stand the *Saathwik*, fair, spotless attributes of love, forbearance, truth and righteousness which are Divine and fostered by God. The combat between the two forces---the down-dragging and the uplifting---knows no armistice. The daily bath ensures cleanliness, the daily battle keeps the evil foes at arm's length beyond capacity to harm.

World is same for the insect and the human being

It is said that during the Kurukshethra battle which lasted for 18 days, Vyaasa had his mind torn with contrition, for the contestants were both of his lineage. So, he could not cast his eyes on the fratricidal carnage! One day, he was so overcome by remorse that he hastened beyond the blood-soaked plain, where another day's holocaust was about to begin. Hurrying along, he saw a spider scurrying forward on the ground! "Why so fast?" inquired the sage; the spider ran off the road, climbed up an ant-hill by its side and from that eminence, it replied, "Know you not that the war chariot of Arjuna is about to pass this way! If I am caught under its wheels, I am down." Vyaasa laughed at this reply; he said, "No eye gets wet when you die! The world suffers no loss when you are killed! You leave no vacuum when you disappear!" The spider was touched to the quick by this insult. It was shaking with rage. It ejaculated, "How is that? You are a bloated sage! You feel that if you die it will be a great loss, whereas I will not be missed at all. I too have wife and children whom I love. I too have a home and a store of food. I too cling to life with as much tenacity as you folk. I have hunger, thirst, grief, pain, joy, delight and the agony of separation from kith and kin. The world is as much in me and for me, as in and for human beings and others."

Vyaasa hung his head and moved on in silence, muttering the line, "*Saamaanyam ethath pasubhir naraani*"---for man and beast, these things are common." But, he told himself, "Enquiry into the Ultimate, yearning for beauty, truth and goodness, awareness of the underlying unity, these attributes of Wisdom are the unique treasures of mankind," and went his way.

Krishna is in the bower and the battlefield

Through this wisdom, man can see the indwelling God in the spider and in every being that exists within the bounds of space. The receptacle may be different, but the Divine content is the same. The taste of sea water will be saline whether you test a truck-load, a bowlful, a potful, or a sip or a drop on the tongue! The taste of the Divine can be experienced in the atom or the cosmos, the friend as well as the foe, the virus and the Universe. This is the Realisation, the Liberation, the Illumination, the Revelation! "*Sarvam Vishnumayam jagath* (the world is God-filled)." This sphere of change is surcharged with the Omnipresent Divine. Sage Thyaagaraaja sang, "O Seethaaraama! Out of your infinite compassion, you shine in the ant and in the Trinity!" Krishna is in the bower and the battlefield, blowing the conch or playing on bewitching flute, wielding whip and wheel, the unseen force behind every thought, word and deed of man everywhere at all times.

Prashaanthi Nilayam, 3.9.1969

18. Elephants and the Lion

THERE is no lack of individuals and institutions in India today devoted to the revival, so far as it lies in their power and along the lines dictated by their intuition, of the precious culture of this land. They toil in the fields of economic progress, moral uplift, or mental integration, social better-ment, political advancement or spiritual enlightenment. The goals and ideals which prompt this activity are laudable and desirable. But all are afflicted by disappointment and exhaustion, soreness or sloth, because the means are either wrong or ineffective.

They have first to demarcate their horizons of action, and define their obligations within those fields. Obligations, not rights! Very often individuals (and even institutions) trespass into the realm of others, compete with fellow workers, and sometimes try to establish superiority, by means fair or foul. Power and position have to be deserved, before they are desired. Those who seek to serve others and promise to cure their ills must have the equipment to diagnose the illness and determine the drug.

Service is a difficult and discriminating process; mere amateur enthusiasm hampers rather than hastens progress. Learning the technique of service, cultivating the impulse to serve, these are steps in equipping a person for leadership.

Service fills the heart with genuine joy

A club has its reputation built by its members; each member as a strand builds up the strength of the institution. If the member is discontented and subject to fits of grumbling, the club cannot be free from anxiety. The Lion's Club is an institution devoted to service. It has come to India from America; but it brings to this land no new message. Its call has echoed in millions of hearts for centuries in this land. The saints and sages of India, and even the Incarnations that God vouchsafed to take in this land, have proclaimed and themselves practised the ideal of service to fellow-beings. Krishna drove the chariot of Arjuna during the fateful days when the fortunes of the Paandavas were decided at the point of the sword. Imagine the Lord of the Universe holding the reins of Arjuna's horses! Note how Hanumaan was elated when he rose to the status of the servant of Raama!

Those of you who have had the privilege of serving your unfortunate brothers and sisters will stand witness to what I am saying now; there is no discipline equal to Service to smother the ego and to fill the heart with genuine joy. To condemn service as demeaning and inferior is to forgo these benefits. A wave of service, if it sweeps over the land, catching every one in its enthusiasm, will be able to wipe off the mounds of hatred, malice and greed that infest the world.

Attune your hearts so that it will vibrate in sympathy with the woes and joys of your fellowmen. Fill the world with Love. Love will warn you against advising another to do something which you yourself are unwilling to do; your conscience will tell you that you are telling a lie! So, before you enroll yourself as a member of a Club dedicated to service, first examine your own mind, see that it is not tarnished by the cobwebs of doubt and the dust of passion. Do not join because some one else is already there, or that it will promote your business, or that it will be an addition to your prestige. Meetings should be convened with an urge to meet, arising out of genuine need, to exchange inspiration and instruction. Do not also be anxious to waste money on dinners; why feed the over-fed? Feed the hungry, the ones who have not had so far the delight that a full meal alone can give.

Intellect crowns you with kingship

Your Club has a very significant name; you are rendering good service to the people. But, I know that you are not deriving from it the sense of satisfaction to the extent anticipated. The Lion is the King of Beasts, the Monarch of the Forest. Man too is a beast, like the jackal, the cheetah, the tiger and the lion. The elephant is the largest of the animals; its footprints are bigger than those of any other. When the elephant walks, it plants its feet so broad and heavy that the footprints of all other animals and denizens of the forest are effaced! And the lion and the elephant are mortal enemies.

There is a deep lesson that Nature teaches you through this: The Mind is the elephant that tramples through the jungle of life, restrained by no fear, regulated by no rule. But, the elephant is dreadfully afraid of the lion. The very sight of the lion fills the elephant with panic! For, the Lion symbolises *Buddhi* (the Intellect). Intellect crowns you with kingship. All have to bend before the throne of Intellect, which confers the highest Bliss. The mind is dumb before the dictates of the intellect; but, before the sense and their demands, it acts as instigator. Make the mind subserve the Intellect; then, the path of man towards God is straightened and smoothed. Lions, as you are, you must investigate the reasons for the defects that you seek to correct, diagnose the ills you attempt to cure and then, discuss the best course of treatment, before actually launching a campaign of service.

Members of certain institutions pay so little attention to the responsibilities that membership involves that they do not know even the aims and objectives. They are in only for the name's sake. This should not be; everyone must be fully aware of the duties, the limits and the lines of action and he must enter with open eyes. Each one must contribute his full share in the discharge of those duties. Your ideal is service; and, so, each person must wholeheartedly co-operate in acts of service.

Zeal and zest are efficient instruments for service

I have noted the work of the Lions in East Africa and in many cities of India. In countries beyond seas, Lions are doing a good job, promoting education and preventing disease. The appalling poverty of our people makes these schemes of service rather too costly and difficult; but do not get discouraged; carry on bravely, to the fullest extent of your resources. Compassion can achieve ends which mere money cannot reach! Zeal and zest are more efficient instruments for service than gifts and donations. They give one man the energy of ten.

There are among you both lawyers and doctors. These can go into the slum areas, and meet the dwellers therein and administer medical and legal help. Or, they can go into some villages and help them with medical and legal advice. Villagers suffer much while trying to secure judicial relief, on account of wrong drafting of documents. They rely on

touts and quacks and discover that they have received
wrong advice, only when it is too late! Extend your
activities to places and people who have no one now to
guide them. Why spend your energies among sections
which are already well served by Government agencies?

Progress is not to be measured by the increase in the
number of members. It is to be judged by the quantity and
the quality of work done. I must draw your attention to
another point. There are many who attribute the unrest in
the country to religion and who prescribe irreligion as the
remedy! The fault lies not in religion, which always insists
on self-control and purity of intentions, brotherhood and
service, but in the human heart which is tainted by greed
and lust. The accusing finger is pointed at the multiplicity
of religions in India, but even people who follow one religion
fight frantically among themselves, even when the religion
directs them to show the other cheek when a slap is
delivered by a foe on one!

Love is the unfailing key to expansion

The followers of one and the same religion may torture
each other and slaughter innocent lives with bestial glee! So,
religion is not responsible at all. The unrest is due to want of
religion, rather than the plethora of religions. It is blind
fanaticism that is to be condemned; not, religion that is
against it. Love of country can also be tainted by fanaticism;
it has led man to destroy by the atom bomb innocent millions
living in another country, hoping thereby to secure the safety
of the country one loves! The mind in which hatred and
egotism grow can never appreciate religion. Is religion the
cause of the calculated cruelty of the atom bomb? No.

The plan and purpose of the ancient religions of
India are to plant the seeds of Love in the human heart
so that they may sprout into saplings of endurance, and

blossom into tolerance, yielding ultimately the fruits of Peace. The pinnacle of Indian thought in *Adhwaitha*, the experience of the One, of the negation of duality. Some countries proceed towards the ideal of individual freedom; others aim at State sovereignty and the suppression of the individual right to freedom. But, Bhaarath has, from time immemorial, sought to infuse in the individual, the lesson that he can be free only when he realises his identity with all—not just the inhabitants of his own state or those who use his own language, or those of his own colour or creed, but all mankind and all beings, alive and inert. Expansion is the key to happiness, and Love is the unfailing key to expansion. Man is kin to all, that is the teaching of *Sanaathana Dharma* (eteral religion).

This idea of kinship is the great inspiration of *Seva*. Emphasise the fact of kinship; your programme of social service will get a move forward. Do not analyse and allot blame; sympathise and shower Love. Serve, in order to heal the agony in your heart; not because the constitution of the Club requires members to serve; not because it brings recognition in high places, or because it is the 'duty' of those who are better off! Serve because you can have no peace unless you serve. It is an inner urge to experience the kinship.

Encourage sense control and self-restraint

Those in charge of administration are not interested in elevating the means; they are keen only on the end, namely, the standard of living. Purity of the means ensures purity of the end. The people, too, are powerless to correct the attitude and motives of the rulers. So, groups of earnest people like you have to alert the rulers and awaken the ruled.

On the plea that the increase of population is harmful to the progress of the country, limiting births artificial means is adopted as a policy and practices are being propagated on a national scale. This is an absurdly wrong step. This is like chopping off the head, since the door is too low and you do not want to enter with a stoop! What you have to do is to discover means of growing more food, by, to give one example, utilising the vast sources of underground water. Artificial means of preventing conception will promote licentiousness and bring down on the country bestial promiscuity. Those who encourage these dangerous tactics must rather encourage sense control and self-restraint through *Yoga* and *Seva*, methods advocated in the scriptures by sages who knew the calamities that are the consequence of irresponsible fatherhood or frustrated motherhood. The innocent, ignorant victims of this campaign, broadening out with so much fanfare, can well be educated to master their lower urges and sublimate them into more beneficial channels. Without mental preparation and determination these artificial methods may cause insanity and other complexes, ill-health and manias.

Through the media of films, books, music and the behaviour of elders, young minds are excited and aroused into indulgence! Through the campaign for Family Planning, they are persuaded to adopt means by which they have no responsibility for the consequences of that indulgence! This is, indeed, burning the future strength and progress of the nation at both ends! The best method for family planning is the ancient one: making man realise through *Saadhana* (spiritual discipline) his innate Divinity. I desire that the doctors among you ponder over the inevitable calamities that will follow the spread of artificial means of family planning, means of escaping the restraints imposed by society, scriptures and culture on the lower instincts of man. You must help to guide the nation along right lines. I bless you that you may succeed in this noble mission of serving the best interests of the nation.

Lions Club, Raajamundry, 10-9-1969

19. Counsel for the chosen

THE *deha* (body) is the temple of God; the *desha* (country, nation) is the *deha* of God. The *deha* is composed of the five elements: Earth, Water, Fire, Wind and Sky. The care of the country is as important as the care of the body. For, happiness and misery, health and disease, pleasure and pain, anxiety and peace are dependent on the health and disease of *desha* (the nation). You have within the next few days, as volunteers at the Prashaanthi Nilayam, the great chance of serving not only yourself but also the country---for people from all the States of the country and even from nations outside its bounds are gathering here for the Dashara Festival. They are all one in heart, in aspiration and in eagerness, whatever the language they speak or the creed they profess! They are clamouring to get this chance to serve as volunteers, but, remember, you alone have had the luck to draw my attention and to receive the blessing. It is therefore a great responsibility.

The service that you can do to the thousands who gather here is not something you render to others, it is

service you render to yourselves. The help is to your own selves.
There was a beggar who once wailed before a rich house for a
mouthful; the master, reclining in an easy chair, drove him
out with harsh abuse. But the beggar persisted. He asked for
some stale food, at least! At this, the daughter-in-law, who was
at her meals in the inner apartments, replied; "My dear fellow!
We are at present eating stale food. The fresh dishes are being
cooked." The beggar knew what she meant; he understood that
the woman was pointing out that the father-in-law by his
insolence and cruelty was preparing for a miserable future, while
his present high standard of living was made possible by the
merit he acquired through charity in previous lives! We eat stale
food, that is to say, the results of the acts in past lives. We also
cook our future meals. So, by this service you are preparing
for a nice banquet in the future, whatever be the food that
you are now eating as a result of past acts!

Life is a long elaborate car-festival

You have come here, and the others too are coming, for
one gain. You must have attended various *ratha-jaathras*
(car-festivals) in our country. The procession will be very
elaborate and long. Drums, cymbals, *bhajans*, bands of
musicians, even clowns will march ahead. Flags and
festoons, arches and pandhals will be erected in the path of
the *rath* or chariot, or temple car. Elephants richly
caparisoned, horses with silver trappings, bullocks and cows,
their horns tipped with silver jingles, and villagers dancing
folk lilts may also be there. But, what is all this for? It is not
for these that the pilgrims come from long distances at great
expense. All this is to highlight the many storied chariot,
which itself is but the vehicle for the Idol, which itself is but
a symbol of the Lord, that every one has come to adore!
Similarly, remember that all the vanities and displays of
life, the clownings and the dances, the miming and the

mumbling, the parades and pastimes which constitute life are only for the adoration of the Lord. Life is a long elaborate *ratha-jaathra*. Every activity must be judged against that background and evaluated. Concentrate on the central theme of life, not on the frills and edges.

Remember that every one coming here has this central theme uppermost in mind; do not discourage them. Do your best to help them achieve their aim, by example as well as by precept, politely administered.

Do not be enslaved by your senses

Every passing minute is a precious gift from God, which you have to use for the best and most lasting benefit. Be happy that you can do so by serving others and catering to their urgent needs. Do not fritter away the minutes in loose talk, retailing scandal, poring over debilitating novels, witnessing films, or mixing with flippant companions. Do not be enslaved by your senses, but bravely resist their demands for indiscriminate freedom. You have the unfailing spring of *Aanandha* in the *Aathman*, which is your reality; why then ruin your health, your peace of mind, running after senses which drag you through the objective world in pursuit of trivial transient joys?

This badge imposes on you great burdens. It will place you prominently before the people; when you ask others to maintain silence, a thousand eyes will be watching, whether you are yourself maintaining silence. You must not exhibit impatience or anger; you must not show any partiality to persons from your village or region, those who speak your language, nor should you show any disrespect or indifference to persons from other regions, those who speak languages other than your own. In all matters, try to discover what action will please me and then behave accordingly. Whoever may or may not watch you, I shall be

with you, wherever you are, now or later, here or elsewhere;
so, be sincere, never try to hoodwink or pretend or deceive.

Pay no attention to the bad in others

This is the introduction for a lifetime of *saadhana* for
each of you. Detachment is the first step in *saadhana*.
Silence helps you not to entangle yourself in the affairs of
others; that is why, it is encouraged as a preliminary. Be
like the ant; when the ant gets a mixture of sand and sugar,
it selects only sugar; it neglects the sand. See only the good
in others; pay no attention to the bad. They may criticise
and cavil at you; but preserve your equanimity and do not
take them to heart! Keep them out; they are sand particles.

Doctors among you who have been allotted the duty of going
round and discovering persons likely to need your attention, must
be extra cordial and considerate. Don't bark questions at the
patients; have patience while listening to their stories; half
the cure is effected by kindness, softness and sympathy.
Vaidhyo Naaraayano Hari, the *Shaasthras* say---"The doctor
is God in human form." It is in that spirit and with that awe
and reverence that people come to you, and receive the drugs
you give. Live up to that estimate of your service! Nowadays,
doctors have lost the art of soft, sweet speech; learn to
speak with compassion; have in your bag the medicines
necessary for the treatment of all types of illness; do not
delay or drift, for want of the drug.

Volunteers must take sick persons to the doctors or
bring the doctor to them, if they cannot be taken. The crow
sits on the back of the buffalo and thrusts its beak into the
raw wound! It has no conception of the pain the beak
causes! Doctors are not aware of the distress they cause, by
neglect or by short temper; volunteers are not aware of the
pain they cause by angry words, or even by a gesture of
contempt or resentment! Imagine what such a gesture can

do for you, if you were in that position---and so avoid it. Always try to put yourselves in the position of the other and, judge your action against that background. Then you will not be wrong.

Do not withhold the sweet word to the sick

Be pure in word and deed, and keep impure thoughts away. I am in every one of you and so, I become aware of your slightest wave of thought. When the clothes become dirty, you have to give them for wash. When your mind is soiled, you have to be born again, for the cleansing operations. The *dhobi* beats the cloth on the hard stone, and draws over it the hot iron, to straighten the folds. So, too, you will have to pass through a train of travail in order to become fit to approach God. See Me as resident in every one; give them all the help you can, all the service they need; do not withhold the sweet word, the supporting hand, the assuring smile, the comforting company, the consoling conversation.

You are now being initiated into a Vow, a status which involves duties and obligations. Krishna wears the *Thilak* of *Kasthuri* (the Dot of Musk) on His forehead indicating the attainment of *Jnaana*. He wears the Pearl of Purity, on His nose, the point where *Dhyaana* is concentrated. He has on His wrist four sacred red strings wound round, to indicate the pledges He has taken for the sake of living beings---to save the good, to punish the wicked, to foster righteousness, to rescue from sin all those who surrender unconditionally to Him. You too have taken a vow today, and worn the badge, as a *kankan* (red string) round the wrist! You must also rescue the distressed, from the unsocial elements that may disturb the even tenor of the Nilayam, and spread joy and content all around you. You have to be examples of *Shaantham* (Equanimity), *Sahanam* (Fortitude) and *Prema*. (Love).

Prashaanthi Nilayam, 11.10.1969

20. *The novel night*

THE *Navaraathri* is the Festival to commemorate the
Victory of Good over Evil. The Embodiment of Divine Power
(*Paraa-shakthi*), in its various manifestations, as *Mahaa-
Saraswathi* (*Saathwik*), as *Mahaa-Lakshmi* (*Raajasik*), as
Mahaa-Kaali (*Thaamasik*) was able to overcome the forces
of vice, wickedness and egoism, during the Nine Days'
struggle and finally, on *Vijaya Dhashami* (the Tenth Day
commemorating Victory), the Valedictory Worship is done.

It is a Festival of Thanksgiving. Gratitude is Divine;
Ingratitude is Demonic. But, while offering the homage of
Gratitude, you must also try to discover who was killed and
who was saved and why. The six enemies of man are eating
into his vitals, embedded in his own inner consciousness.
They are the demons to be killed. They are lust (*kaama*),
anger (*krodha*), greed (*lobha*), attachment (*moha*), pride
(*madha*) and malice (*maathsarya*). They reduce man to the
level of a demon. They have to be overpowered and
transmuted, by the supreme alchemy of the Divine Urge.
Then, the nine nights of struggle will become new, a new

type of night, devoted to the purification of the mind, and the illumination of the soul---the night described in the Geetha as 'the day of the worldly.' What is clear and attractive to the ordinary man is uninteresting and unknown to the *yogi*; what is clear and attractive to the *yogi* is uninteresting and unknown to the worldly man. That is the nature of this topsy-turvy world.

Do everything for the Glory of God

To celebrate the *Nava-raathri*, new as well as nine (*nava* means both 'new' and 'nine'), at the Prashaanthi Nilayam is indeed a rare chance, replete with wonder and joy. For this is the Abode of Peace, the Peace that ensues when the six enemies are destroyed for ever. The *Prashaanthi* Flag which will now be hoisted is the symbol of this consummation---the conquest by man of the six enemies and the illumination within him of the Flame of Wisdom, installed in the Lotus of the Heart. It is the Flag of *Swa-raaj* (Dominion over Oneself), the true Independence, when you can genuinely claim to be master of the realm most intimately related to you. It is the Flag that flutters in the breeze of *Aanandha*; the Flag that announces the arrival of Inner Splendour. It is the Flag that heralds the Dawn of the highest wisdom and the deepest peace.

Man is proud that he is flying far into the sky and even landing on the Moon; but, he is incapable of living at peace with himself or his neighbours. His life on earth is full of fear and anxiety; but, he proclaims without shame that he is the summit of creation! He does not know how to put down the fire that burns within himself; but he is able to destroy entire cities by fire, emanating from bombs!

Swa-raaj means full mastery over your senses, mind and intelligence, through the recognition of the *Aathma*. You must not be dependent on another for services that you can well do yourself. What is the use of tiring out a servant in subserving your wishes and yourself sitting lazily in meditation? Engage in activity, devote yourself in worshipful acts, do everything for the glory of God---that is far more fruitful than the 'meditation' which you are relying on.

Just as a thermometer indicates the heat of the body, your talk, conduct, and behaviour indicate your mental equipment and attitudes, and show how high is the fever of worldliness that afflicts you. These have to be *Saathwik* (pure), untinged by passion of emotions like hate or pride. Talk in peace, promoting peace in others. What is the use of *japa* and *dhyaana*, when your talk and conduct are not even human? How can you hope to approach the divine while grovelling in the slush of the bestial? This is the first day of *Dashara* Festival and so, resolve this day to cleanse the mind of impurities, so that you can imbibe the inspiration it is intended to convey.

Aspirants for mental peace have also to reduce the luggage they have to care for; the more the luggage, the greater the bother. Objective possessions and subjective desires, both are handicaps in the race for realisation. A house cluttered with lumber will be dark, dusty, and without free movement of fresh air, it will be stuffy and suffocating. The human body too is a house; do not allow it to be cluttered with curios, trinkets, trash, and superfluous furnishings. Let the breeze of holiness blow as it wills through it; let not the darkness of blind ignorance desecrate it. Life is a bridge over the sea of change; pass over it, but do not build a house on it.

Hoist the Prashaanthi Flag, on the temple, that is your heart. Follow the prescription it teaches---subdue the six enemies that undermine the natural bliss in man, ascend the *Yoga* stage when the agitations are stilled and allow the Splendour of the Divinity within (the *Aathma*) to shine forth, embracing all for all time.

Prashaanthi Nilayam, 12.10.1969

21. Seaworthy boat

To many it might appear strange that in this *Aanandha-nilaya* (Abode of Bliss), there exists an *Aarogya Nilaya* (Abode of Health) or Hospital. They may wonder why prominence is given to bodily health, in a place that is dedicated to the health of the spirit. But, for attaining the Four Aims of Human life, *Dharma* (Righteousness), *Artha* (Prosperity), *Kaama* (Fulfilment of Desires) and *Moksha* (Liberation from bondage), the basic requirement is health of body and mind. Disease means feeling uneasy, disturbed, on account of the upsetting of one's temper or balance or equilibrium, which affects the physical as well as mental condition. This happens for two reasons: faulty *Aahaara* (food) and faulty *Vihaara* (activities).

It is wise to prevent disease than run after remedies after it has happened or grown beyond control. Man does not attend to precautionary measures; he allows things to worsen and then the disease is aggravated by fear, uncertainty and anxiety. There is an axiom believed in by men of old, which says: 'One meal a day makes a *Yogi*, two

meals a day make a *Bhogi* and three meals a day make a
Rogi.' Yogi is the contented God-centred man. *Bhogi* is the
man revelling in sensual pleasure. *Rogi* is the man ridden
by illness. Yes. The quantity of food intake by the well-to-do
is now much beyond essential requirements. Over-eating
has become a fashion.

The breakfast does not serve to break any fast, for,
there has been no fasting at all! It is as good as a full meal.
Lunch is pressed in and consists of many dishes, chosen for
the palate rather than to assuage hunger. Tea is tea only
in name; it includes rather heavy fare, out of all proportion
to the needs of the body. Dinner at night is the heaviest
meal and includes the largest variety and so one goes to
bed, weighted with unwanted stuff, to roll from side to side,
in a vain effort to get a few minutes of sleep. The shortage
of food grains is mainly due to bad and wasteful eating
habits; it can be set right, and people can live longer and
more healthily, if only they eat the minimum, rather than
fill themselves with maximum.

Regular prayers will give strength and courage

Regular prayers twice a day will give strength and
courage, which can withstand illness. The Grace of God will
confer mental peace and so, good sleep and rest for the
mind. Feel that you are a hundred per cent dependent on
God; He will look after you and save you from harm and
injury. When you go to bed, offer thankful homage to Him
for guiding and guarding you throughout the day. When a
friend offers you a cigarette or some one gives you a glass
of water, you say immediately, "Thank you;" how much
more gratitude should you evince to God who watches you
and wards off all harm threatening to overwhelm you.
Activity must be dedicated to God, the Highest Good. Then,
it will provide health of body and mind.

The body is a chariot, wherein God is installed, being taken along in procession. Let us consider some points on which we have to be vigilant, in order to avoid breakdowns on the road: Fast one day in the week. This is good for the body as well as for the country. Do not eat a dozen plantains, half a dozen *puris* and drink a quart of milk and call it a fast! Take only water, so that all the dirt is washed away. Do not crave for fruit juice or other liquids. Even physical machinery is given rest; they cannot run for ever, continuously. What then shall we say of this delicately organised human body! It is not a sign of culture to overvalue the body, by over indulging in its whims. It is a sign of barbarism.

Birds and beasts have better eating habits

The older generation in this land used to take some quantity of rice soaked in curds, first meal in the morning. It is good *Saathwik* food; or, they drank some *raagi* gruel, which is equally good. Cattle are better; dogs have better eating habits. If a dog has fever, it will refuse food; but, man ignores even the warnings of the doctor and eats on the sly! Through dieting alone, birds and beasts set their health allright! But, man lives on tablets and pills and injections, after venturing into forbidden realm, so far as eating and drinking are concerned. Drink large quantities of water, boiled and cooled, not during meals, but some time before and after. Only the healthy person can afford to forget the body and dedicate his thoughts to God, and derive *Aanandha* therefrom.

The mind is the eleventh sense and like the other ten, one must reduce it to the status of an obedient instrument, in the hands of the intellect. Eat at regular intervals, according to a well-established time-table. Move about and fill the day with activity, so that food is well digested. Develop biting hunger, before sitting down for a meal.

Now, many do not know what it is to be hungry or thirsty. Wait until you get the call, before you load the stomach again. The rich are under a great handicap, in this respect. And women, who are petted so much that they feel physical work to be demeaning!

Contentment is the best tonic

Illness is the inevitable result of idleness and indulgence; health is the inevitable consequence of a tough hard life. If every one decides to carry on all personal services themselves, rather than depend on servants or helpers , the health situation will definitely improve and hospitals will have much less work. Keeping the mind fixed on God and good ideas and things also helps health. Keep the eye, ear, tongue, hands and feet under restraint. Don't read enervating or exiciting stuff; don't attend film shows which exhaust or inflame the mind. Don't lose faith in yourself, you are the Divine encased in the body. Contentment is the best tonic; why inflict on yourself the disease of greed and consume tonics to get strength, and to hanker further? Use the body as a boat to cross the ocean of life, with devotion and detachment as the two oars.

Do not spend much thought on the body; some people worry always about health, and they are never satisfied with the care they bestow on the body. Be in the sun; let the sun's rays penetrate into the home, let them fall upon the body for some time, let them warm and illumine clothes and food; that will suffuse them with health.

There are some who are puzzled at the sight of a hospital here. They imply that everything here should be done through some miracle or some strange inexplicable manner! It also implies that no one who has come here should fall ill or die. I have no desire that you should live; or fear that you may die. It is you that decide your condition. All have to die, sooner or later. No one will be anxious to have the same dress on for years and years. Death is but the casting off of old clothes. When even *Avathaars* leave the body after the Task is fulfilled, how can man be saved from inevitable dissolution? The Hospital is for those who believe in the doctor and in drugs. It is faith that matters, that cures. It also serves to accommodate those who are too ill to move about, but, yet come over to this place for cure. Those who are in the Hospital will also hear the *Pranava*, the *Sankeertan* and the *Bhajan* and benefit by the spiritual vibrations that fill the air in this Prashaanthi Nilayam.

Prashaanthi Nilayam, 12.10.1969

You should cultivate an attitude of inseparable attachment to the Lord, who is your very self. If He is a flower, you should feel yourself a bee that sucks its honey; if He is a tree, be a creeper that clings to it; if a cliff, then feel that you are a cascade running over it; if He is the sky, be a tiny star that twinkles in it; above all, be conscious of the truth that you and He are bound by Supreme Love. If you feel this acutely, not with the gross intelligence, but with the subtle intelligence, then, the journey will be quick and the goal can be won.

Sathya Sai Baaba

22. Sign and symptom of glory

MAN has to journey over the road that lies over pleasure and pain, grief and joy; the journey can be smooth, only when he resorts to wisdom, devotion and detachment as his equipment for the travail of travel. These are available to him in large measure, provided he will listen to the experience of elders, as written in scripture or as related personally all around him; he can also get acquainted with them, if only he sits down silently for a while and watches the flow of events and the passage of the caravan of life.

The child rolls unconcerned in urine and faeces, because it is unaware of the dirt and the disgust; but, as it grows in experience and wisdom, it learns that it is shameful and dangerous to grovel in dirt. Similarly, man in his ignorance rolls in sensory absurdities; he has then some excuse for not knowing better. Later, however, if he does not learn by experience and keep away from the nauseating habits and pursuits that demean his intelligence and powers of discrimination, he becomes the target of ridicule. He is a danger to himself and others.

The noun collects many adjectives, the innocent individual gets many attributes attached to it, that deface its purity! The doctor is incapable of diagnosing the illness—he can judge only the equilibrium between the three body humours of *vaatha, pittha* and *kapha* (wind, bile, and phlegm; only the Divine Doctor, (*Vaidhyo Naaraayano Harih*) the expert in the inner sheaths of the individual—the *Vijnaanamaya kosha*, the *Aanandha-maya kosha* (wisdom and bliss)—can distinguish between the *Gunas* (qualities) and their influences on character and activity.

Merit is when you do good to another

Enthusiasm to progress in the spiritual field and earn mental peace thereby is on the increase in recent years; this is another evidence of the Grace that the *Avathaar* (divine incarnation) sheds. There is enormous interest, not only in India, but all over the world in the methods adopted by the *Rishis* (sages) of this land to acquire *shaanthi* (peace), through *Prema* (Love) and through *Yoga, Dharma* and *Sathya* (communion with God, virtue and truth). Ten or fifteen years ago, attendance at discourses on religious subjects was very sparse, only a handful of old men and women! But now, we see thousands and lakhs, coming from long distances and sitting through long hours, eager and expectant! And, a large majority are youth! Youth is eager to share the heritage of the past, so that they may build a better future for themselves.

The word *Hindhu* means those who keep away from the path of violence, away of from inflicting injury on others; *Hin* (*Hinsa*-injury, violence); *dhu* (*dhura*—away, distant). The *Shaasthras* declare that the essence of all the 18 *Puraanas* so highly revered in India is: Merit is when you do good to another; sin is when you do evil to another. When you are fixed in this path, you will welcome all faiths and religions as kith and kin; all faiths attempt to train man along this path. Muslims, Christians, Buddhists, Jews, Parsis all aspire to win the same Illumination, through the cleansing of the mind by means of good works. The seeds of all these are in the *Sanaathana Dharma* of the *Vedhaantha* (concluding philosophical portion of sacred scriptures).

Just as the Congress has a number of splinter parties like the SSP, PSP and even the Communist Party, so too other faiths are but the right, left or centre, of the *Sanaathana Dharma* of India. That *Dharma* examines all possible approaches to the Divine and arranges them in the order in which they can be utilised by the aspirant, according to the level of equipment and attainment. When a tree first shoots forth from the seed, it comes up with a stem and two incipient leaves! But, later, when it grows, the trunk is one, and the branches are many! Each branch may be thick enough to be called a trunk; but, one should not forget that the roots send food as sap through one single trunk. God, the same God, feeds the spiritual hunger of all nations and all faiths, through the common sustenance of truth, virtue, humility and sacrifice.

Vedhic Dharma is the grandfather of all religions

Last May, when I was in Bombay for the Annual Day of the Dharmakshethra, we had a gathering of intellectuals at Dr. K.M. Munshi's place, when a number of Vice-Chancellors, doctors, advocates and professors were eager to meet me. The meeting turned out to be a question and answer session, for about six hours!

One question was about this: the different faiths that drag men into diverse, divergent paths! I told them: No one knows exactly when the *Vedhas* were collated in their present form. Bala Gangadhar Thilak surmised that it must have happened about 13,000 years ago; others bring the date down to 6,000 years ago, but, all are agreed that it was beyond at least 4,000 years! And, Buddha is a historical figure, who lived about 2,500 years ago. Christ was born 1969 years ago, and Islam was formed 600 years later. So, chronologically as well as logically, the inference is correct, that the *Vedhic Dharma* is the grandfather, Buddhism is the Son, Christianity the grandson, and Islam the great-grandson. If there is any misunderstanding between them it is but a family affair. The ancestral property of which all are co-sharers is the same.

Another question was about the Atom Bombs, and whether India should not endeavour to acquire the same. I replied that it is no shame that we have not made one; it is a source of pride that we have not made one. We do not need one to get the senses of security. The Five Paandava Brothers were led by the eldest of them, aptly named Dharmaraaja, the Upholder of Right. His brother Bheema was the mightiest warrior of those days, who used to wield a mace, which shook the earth when it was planted by him on the ground. He wrestled with the gigantic Keechaka and slew him. He was unexcelled in intellectual and physical strength. Another brother, Arjuna was the master bowman of the age, armed with some of the most potent arrows that the Gods themselves bad bestowed on him, in appreciation of his valour and his faith. But, these two brothers acted as if they were but the limbs of the eldest brother; they never deviated from the path of righteousness laid down by Dharmaraaja.

Let 'service' be the slogan for this nation

I told that gathering that so long as India stuck to the path of *Dharma* (righteousness), Russia, which is the Bheema of the day and America, the Arjuna of the day will revere this land and learn from it the means of securing mental peace and security. For, their present power and pride are the manifestations of an indwelling fear, an unallayed agony eating the vitals. The Paandavas were therefore blessed by the Lord, to come through all the travail that assailed them. The Paandavas were so righteous that, when they found their enemies, the Kauravas, kidnapped by the Gandharva tribe, they rushed to rescue them (!) for they knew that there was no other way of getting them released from their fell hands! That is the role that you too should play. Service—let that be the slogan for this nation. Service, not for those who have many to serve them, the wherewithal to help themselves, but, for the diseased in the hospitals who have no one to nurse them, nourish them or give them a smile or a flower, or write a letter home for them.

Giving and sharing doubles the joy

One day when a number of sages met, they had a discussion on the code of conduct for women. There were some women present; they desired to know the duties of the housewife. The women said that they were filled with *Aanandha* (happiness) when they gave away, and not when they received and accumulated! The happiest moments of motherhood were when the mother feeds her baby, her own essential self, at her breast, allowing it to imbibe her own health through its lips. Another woman said that she felt more joy when she served the dishes that she cooked to others, her husband, her children, the guests, rather than when she partook of them, herself. It is in giving that the joy lies, not in receiving. No one can enjoy eating even the richest meal alone! Sharing doubles the joy.

I want to tell you that the *Aanandha* (bliss) you derive from service is something you can never get through any other activity. The thrill that a kind word, a small gift, a good gesture, a sign of sympathy, a sign of compassion can bring about on a distressed heart is something that is beyond words to describe.

The *Vedhas* teach man that all are kin; that all are divine. They emphasise that God is Love. It is to preserve this valuable heritage, to propagate it, and save the world from the waves of hatred and violence that are overwhelming it, that the All India Prashaanthi Vidhwanmahaasabha (the great Assembly of Scholars) has been formed. It will instil reverence for the ancient temples of this land, wherefrom spiritual vibrations spread over the entire community. They were museums of art, promoters of poetry, schools of *Vedhic* studies, integrators of caste and instruments of moral upliftment. The *Sabha* will endeavour to foster these activities and encourage other kindered organisations having the ideal of fostering the universal values of religion.

Today man is denying himself the boon of peace

By peace, Western countries mean the interval between two wars, when vigorous efforts are made to avenge the insult of defeat, and consolidate the spoils of victory and prepare for the next round! That is no peace! When man thinks good, and speaks good, and does good, "*Shaanthi* (peace) will ensue, but, he now speaks good, though he thinks evil and proposes to do evil! He ignores the principle of Immortality that is his core, the principle of Love that is the life-blood of the human community; he denies himself the boon of peace and rushes towards destruction. Destroying others he destroys himself.

It is only in the contemplation of the beauty, majesty and Omnipresence of God that one can be at peace. This hour when you have been sitting so tightly packed before me here, you have had no other thoughts than these, I am sure. Make your heart a Prashaanthi Nilayam (abode of Supreme Peace), by the recollection of God's glory and of your being a sign and symptom of that Glory. The Minister was saying that he wishes to do something for the Nilayam. He said that he would personally approach his colleagues in the Ministry and see that the road to this place is improved soon. The body craves the comfort of a macadamised or tarred

road; but, the heart prefers the road of purity and humility,
so that it may reach the Goal of Mergence with God. I am
more interested in that Road; I am not enthusiastic about
the tarred road, for, that would make the journey to this
place easier and so even the little discipline of slow, careful
driving that is now imposed upon people coming here will
disappear!

Learn to bear with some little difficulty, while
coming here. Life is not all smooth riding. It is a series
of ups and downs. Bhaarath has taught and practised
the art of smooth travel, for centuries. Learn that art and
be at peace.

Prashaanthi Nilayam, 14.10.1969

Being in company of the holy is like the bit and bridle for the wanton steed, the anicut and canals for the raging flood. The value of holy places, consists in just this; kindred spirits congregate there and contribute to the deepening of spiritual yearning. You can take sweet and sustaining counsel together in such places and strengthen your faith and devotion.

Sathya Sai Baaba

23. Forsake the fete of fancy

WHY does man wail when he arrives into the world, whimper throughout his life and groan out, into the beyond, lamenting that his sojourn here was a waste of years? Man does so, because he is unaware of his glory, of his high destiny! He is the Divine poured into the human mould, just as everything else, alive or inert, is; but, it is the privilege of man alone, to be able to become aware of this precious truth! This is the message of the *Upanishadhs* to man. This message is echoed by the scriptures, and in the declarations of countless saints. Yet, man turns a deaf ear to it, perhaps, due to his own misfortune created by his own misdeeds in past lives. He can derive *Aanandha* (Divine Bliss) through the contemplation of his Divinity, or the Divine as represented by all that he sees, hears, tastes, touches or smells outside himself. *"Sarvam Brahmamayam"*—Brahman is immanent in all. What an inexhaustible source of *Aanandha* lies inside or outside you! Only you have to develop the mind that will respond to the call, that will recognise the Truth. The baby in the cradle is the very picture of *Aanandha*; when it

cries out of grief, we run towards it, for, it is against its
nature to be sad. Man too is essentially Bliss. Misery is
alien to his make- up.

Recognising the immanence of the Divine, one has to
dedicate all acts to the Divine. What is the act, when you
analyse it deeply? It is the manipulation of the Divine by
the Divine, for the sake of the Divine through the skill
endowed by the Divine; there is no I or mine in it, except the
Universal I and the Divine My.

Keep the mind away from vice and greed

Dedication is to be carried out in various ways. Take
the food that we consume. Offer it to God, before you
partake of it. Then it is rendered pure and potent. Any act
done for the glorification of God is thereby rendered pure
and potent. It is incapable of harming the doer, the
beneficiary, or society, for, it is saturated with Love, which
is God. God is the director of this puppet show, the
manipulator of the strings. Go behind the screen and see
Him. It is now hiding Him; you have only to peep behind a
flower, peer behind a cloud, to see Him pulling the string,
to show us the beauty, to show us the darkness of heavy
moisture. So also, you have only to peep behind your
thoughts, to peer behind your feelings; you will find there
the Inner Motivator! This process of looking inwards is
taught in the *Yogashaasthra* (science of *yoga*) of India. But,
you must approach teachers, who are pure and selfless, not,
those who make up for their ignorance by stunts and feats.

If you do not get such a teacher, mere meditation on
the Name and Form of God (whatever Name and Form that
appeals to you) is enough. Or, even the recollection of the
Name and the Glory is enough. Keeping the mind away
from vice and greed is important. The heart should be kept
tender and compassionate. It is not age that matters; a

person may be old, but, his heart may be fresh and tender, full of enthusiasm for service and willingness to sacrifice. That will ensure your getting the passport to the spiritual realm. Divinity is only the terminus of the journey of human life, like the ripe fruit being the terminus of the journey from bud through blossom, from blossom to the fruiting, the sour bitter fruit to the sweet juiceful ripeness. Grace is the sunlight which will ripen the fruit. *Saadhana* is the sap which rises from the earth. Both are needed by the tree, in order that it may yield fruit.

Seven steps to be mastered in meditation

Grace is showered on those who seek. Knock, and the door shall be opened; ask, and food will be served; search, and the treasure will be yours. You may complain, Yes! Swaami! We have been knocking, asking, and searching, since years...but, the door is yet unopened, the food is still not forthcoming, the treasure is still beyond our reach! But, let me ask you this. You have been asking the devil not the deity, knocking at the devil's door and digging for the treasure at the devil's realm. The devil's realm is the objective world, outer nature, *Prakrithi*! She is a clever enchantress! You have been propitiating her, believing that she can confer peace and *Aanandha*! She tantalises you and leads you from one disappointment to another. She enhances your ego and sense of achievement, until you collapse from swollen head! You are knocking at the wrong door---the door of hell, which is ever open! You are searching for paltry pleasure, not permanent treasure!

You tell me, "Swaami! I have been practising intense meditation since 50 years, but, I have yet to gain concentration. This is a shameful confession. *Dhyaana* is the seventh in the series of steps, leading to the eighth *Samaadhi* (conquest of the Mind). Unless you have secured a strong foothold on the six previous steps, you will slide back from *Dhyaana*, however many years you may try to stick to it. The first step is the control of the senses, the second is the control of the emotions and impulses. The third is the mastery of balance and equipoise, the fourth is the regulation of breathing and movements of the vital airs, the fifth is the prevention of outer influences from deviating the mind, the sixth is one-pointed attention on one's own progress, and then, we come to real *Dhyaana*---meditation on one's Reality---which easily leads to its realisation in *Samaadhi*. Without the preliminary rungs, you cannot hop straight on to seventh! And then, skip on to the eighth!

Reduce your 'luggage' to make life's journey safer

Reduce the luggage you carry about, when on the journey of life. Remember, all that is not 'you' is luggage! You are not the body. So, the body is an item of luggage. The mind, senses, the intelligence, the imagination, the desires, the plans, the prejudices, the discontent, the distress---all are items of luggage. Jettison them soon, to make your travel lighter, safer and more comfortable. Learn this lesson watching the great, who are humble and simple. They are the elders whom you should admire and follow. They are the people who bring forth your tears when they pass away; there are others who bring forth your tears, when they pass your way! They are to be avoided.

God makes himself aware to beasts and birds, rather than man, who has strayed into the wilderness. Recently at Dharmaavaram, a *jutka* (horse-drawn cart) full of men and luggage was being driven towards the railway station, the driver beating the horse mercilessly on the back and neck, so that it may run fast. A bearded old man, fair and rosy in health, was passing that way. He accosted the driver and said, "Here! Don't hold the reins so tight. Leave them free, hold them loose! The horse will then run fast." The driver retorted. "You keep quiet! I know my horse better." One of the men inside the *jutka* said, "I don't care!" The driver then heard a voice (it was the horse that spoke). "He is Krishna, who drove the horses of Arjuna's chariot. He knows all about horses!" The driver thought that the voice belonged to some one among his fare. He replied, looking into the *jutka*. "He may know all about Arjuna's horses; but, what does he know about mine?"

The *Gopees* felt that a bee can sympathise with their pangs of separation from Krishna, more than any human messenger. They asked the bee to intercede with the Lord, on their behalf. Pray to Him, to wear the garland of my adoration, one *Gopee* asked the bee. Another wanted it to ask Krishna to illumine the darkness of her heart. Raadha asked it to pray to Krishna to make the desert sands of her heart sprout into green, so that His Feet may tread thereon, light and soft.

Mere scholarship will not lead to mergence with God

Offer to God the clear calm *Maanasa* lake; or even if the mind is wayward and freakish like the monkey, offer it to God, as Shankaraachaarya did. He prayed to Shiva, "Lord! I have with me just the thing you need, when you go a-begging. I have a monkey, most mischievous, jumping at everybody and everything that attracts its fancy! Take it with you; and like the beggars who carry a monkey about with them, you will be a more welcome beggar among the children of the villages you frequent!"

Give the mind over to God, pure or puerile. Be sincere in your yearning and in your *Saadhana*. Formal scholarship and outward conformity are poor substitues for real genuine devotion. Shankaraa-chaarya was going along the streets of Vaaranasi, when he saw in a small hermitage a monk poring over a book of grammer! He took pity on the ageing scholar and warned him that when the end drew near, his scholarship will not save him from perdition, or take him to the goal of mergence with God. So, he asked him to adore God, and fill himself with thoughts Divine. That is the proper way to deal with life, not frittering it away as a fate of fancy.

Prashaanthi Nilayam, 15-10-1969

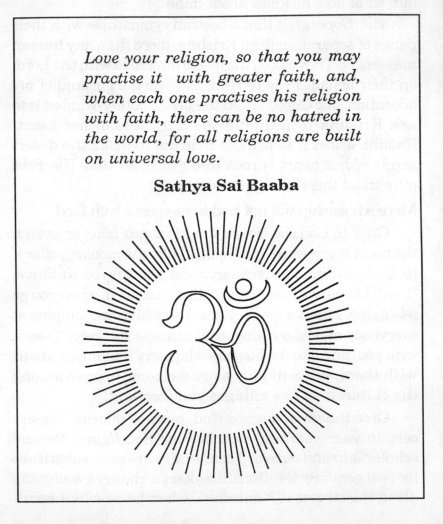

Love your religion, so that you may practise it with greater faith, and, when each one practises his religion with faith, there can be no hatred in the world, for all religions are built on universal love.

Sathya Sai Baaba

24. Exercise in futility

CULTIVATE comradeship with the good, develop compassion for the distressed, foster the feeling of elation at the happy and prosperous, and deepen indifference towards the evil-minded---this is the ancient, well-tried prescription for a calm peaceful life. God will bless such men and award them Grace. The Name of God when uttered with sincere joy has great influence on the mind of man. It is like moonlight, for the waves of the inner Ocean in man. For, it is God echoing from within, the call of God from without! But, lo, the fascination exerted by science—which deals with the objective world, with things and events that can be measured, weighed or calculated by means of ascertainable categories of thought—has led man into the dreary wastes, in search of Joy! Chandramouli Shaasthry was telling you now about the *manthras*, which when repeated in faith and with full knowledge of implications, can endow you with mysterious experiences of the Divine. That is to say, the *manthra* enables you to be in the proximity of the Divine that is drawn near by the potency of the formula when charged with your own mental current.

What is *manthra*? *Man* (*manana*: continued reflection on latent meanings), *thra* (*thraana*: the act of saving, of enabling one to cross over sorrow). What are the conditions under which the mind can charge the *manthra* with the required potency? The first and foremost one is: one-pointedness. Now, the mind is a very poor instrument, for, it is blunt. It runs after too many objects and objectives. The moment you persuade it to fix its attention on God, it wanders into the cinema hall, the bazaar, the Card Room of your Club, etc. It will seldom agree to dwell on the vast magnificence of the Divine; when you direct it to the Divine, it will behave as if you are inviting it to face the deluge or to counter the horrors of Hell!

Faith in Divinity is essential to dwell upon God

The faith in Divinity essential for any exercise to dwell upon Him, is absent. That faith can come only slowly, by association with the godly, by reading the lives and experiences of godly persons, and by gaining experience oneself. *Naama sankeerthan* (singing of God's Names) induces faith, very quickly. In the beginning, the name has to be recited, willy nilly, as a routine; later, the taste will draw you into the habit; the recitation will yield unfailing joy. We speak of the Lotus of the Heart! Why? Because, the Lotus grows up in and from water and blooms in the sun. The heart too draws sustenance from *Bhakthi* (Devotion) and blooms through *Jnaana* (Wisdom).

Most of the Names of the Divine have but two letters or syllables; the significance of the number, two, (Raama, Krishna, Hara, Hari, Datta, Shakthi, Kaali, etc.) is, that the first syllable represents *Agni* (Fire principle), which burns up accumulated demerit or sin, and the second, represents the *Amritha* principle, the Restorative, the Refreshing, the Reformation force. The two processes are necessary;

removal of obstructions and construction of the structure.

Krishna, the Lord, was fostered by Yasodha, but, she did not know where He was born! He was loved and treated as if He were her own son; that is to say, her love was pure and unaffected by selfish considerations. The parable is to be understood thus: Born in the region of the navel, the Divine vitality was later preserved and developed on the tongue (in Gokula, by Nandha and Yasodha), by constant repetition of the Name.

The Raama Principle is the Principle of Love, that descended from Heaven, as the gift of the Gods, as a result of the great sacrifice. *Raama* means Delight! Nothing delights more than one's own innate self, and so, *Raama* is also known as *Aathmaa-Raama*. How then could Bharatha accept to usurp the throne, of which Raama is the rightful heir? He and Shathrughna were at the Kekaya capital, when Raama was exiled, and Dhasharatha died heartbroken at the separation. News was sent to him, and when he entered the palace, unaware of the double tragedy that had cast its gloom over the city, he sensed some calamity. Vasishtha, the family preceptor, advised him to ascend the throne, for, the empire was suffering an interregnum!

Bharatha's example of love for Raama the Lord

Bharatha appealed that he be allowed to go to "the God of my Prayers, the Lord who receives the homage of my unceasing adoration." Vasishtha told him that it was his father's command, and his preceptor's counsel that he sit enthroned as Ruler. Bharatha replied that the request was proof of the extreme hatred that the parents, the people, the preceptor and everyone in Ayodhya had towards him, for, had they loved him, they would not have pressed him to do such a mean sin.

Bharatha stood before Sage Vasishtha with folded palms; he prayed, "Is it just, is it fair, that you should burden me with the sovereignty over a kingdom, which slew my father, widowed my mothers, exiled my dearest brother whom I value more than my very breath, to the demon-ridden jungle, with his dearly beloved queen and which finally brought indelible disgrace on my mother? My empire is the realm which Raama rules over, namely, my heart, which is too small to contain His glory." Bharatha's name itself signifies that he is saturated with love of Raama. (*Bha*---means *Bhagavaan*, the Lord Raama; *ratha*---means pleased by, happy over, attached to).

Education has hardened the human heart

Let the Love for the Lord grow in you, as it did in Bharatha. Let that sense of adoration, which discarded even a throne, flourish in you. Then, you can be of great use to your country, your culture, your society, your religion and your community. Or else, all this bother that you have undergone, to attend *Sathsang*, to listen to spiritual discourse, to meet spiritual masters, study spiritual texts, etc., will be a colossal exercise in futility. The system of education laying empahsis on literacy, skills, conformity and material progress has hardened the human heart into another weapon, in the stock of military hardware! His intellect has been blunted by constant iteration of lies; awe and reverence which fed the holy emotions in man have been condemned as out-dated! Holy men, holy places and rivers are ridiculed. India which was for ages the playground of the Gods and the nursery of saints and the *Guru* of mankind has now become a beggar at the doors of the very people who clamour for *Vedhaanthic* Light!

Know the splendour of that light, and fly unto it, as high as your wings can lift you---the wings of *Bhakthi* and *Shraddha* (Devotion and Steadfastness).

The Shaasthry said that it is an impossible task---
the description of the miracles of Swaami. How can any
one describe unless he understands the mystery? How
can a man on the shore calculate the waves of the sea?
He can never count the total. For him, the wave with
which he began his count is the first and the wave with
which he left off count is the last. Listen, ruminate and
follow the advice---that is enough *saadhana* for you.

The first and foremost of my directions is: Revere
your parents especially, the mother. There was once a
place, which was hit by a hurricane so wildly that all the
houses were razed to the ground, and people had
nothing to eat and nowhere to lay their heads. Among the
worst hit were a mother and her two sons. The elder boy
was a gem of virtue; he felt responsible for the safety and
care of the family, for, he loved his mother, and sought
to win her love and blessings more than anything else.

A true devotee must first revere his mother

You speak of *Bhaaratha maatha*, the Motherland;
every mother is of the same breath, of the same lineage.
The mother with the younger child was going out begging
and keeping alive on the little they could get from the
famine-stricken land. Soon, she found that she was too
weak even to walk a few steps and so, the elder son had to
go a-begging all alone, to feed the family. He said, falling
at her feet, that he would do what she was doing and collect
food for all. He wanted that she should not over-exert, and
worsen her health. How could they live on mere handfuls?
The son too was rendered weak. With faint voice and
fainter steps, he moved towards a zamindar's house and
called out for a morsel. The lady of the house called him in
and led him before a leaf, whereon she served some food.
But, he tottered into an upright position, and fell plump

on the floor. The zamindar came running into the room and placed his ear, near the dying boy's mouth, so that he could catch the last words that emerged from his lips. He was saying, 'No, No! First, she must be given food; my turn comes next.' You may be able to pay back any debt; but, the debt you owe your mother, you never can repay. Those who claim to be devotees of God must have this credential: they must revere the mother!

Prashaanthi Nilayam, 16.10.1969

__Bhakthi__ or devotion to God is not to be judged or measured by rosaries or candles, daubings on the forehead or matted hair or jingles on the ankles; purity of motives and intentions is essential, so that prema *which is the one component of* bhakthi *does not leak out of the heart.*

Sathya Sai Baaba

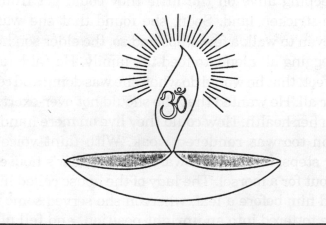

25. Assert with every breath

THE Shaasthry explained to you the power and influence of Time on human affairs, taking examples from epics as well as from history. What is good today may be bad tomorrow; what is practicable today may be impracticable tomorrow. Time has a way of making habits and customs out-dated, anachronistic. What gives grief today may yield joy tomorrow. Going to school is an unpleasant task for the child; but, later, he is thankful for having been forced to attend classes while young! Seetha renounced Ayodhya, the palace and all the dreams of happiness she had, and followed Raama into the forest, when he was exiled; but, the sight of a golden deer aroused her latent desires, and she had to face a series of calamities as a consequence of the emergence of 'attachment' to worldly objects! Time had conspired to keep the roots of desire alive in her heart.

The *Raamaayana* teaches also another lesson. The search for Seetha is symbolic of the secret of self-realisation, in the field of experience. Raama, when she was recovered, recovered the wisdom of self-realisation,

now confirmed by experience. *Jnaana* had become
Anubhava-jnaana. The *Raamaayana* teaches that, when
a person is yearning for the precious goal of self-realisation,
all the forces of Nature and all Creation will help him and
render all assistance. Monkeys, birds, squirrels, and even
bounders and rocks were his comrades in the task. Aim
high, resolve on the supremest adventure---everything will
be set right to lead you on, to the goal.

The world is the triple complex of *Gunas*

In fact, you are urged on towards this adventure by your
very breath, which repeats 21,600 times a day *Soham* (He-I),
emphasising the identity of the Indweller with the Principle
that is Immanent in the Universe. You may declare with
your tongue, "There is no God," but, the breath repeats, *SO*
as it goes in and *HAM* as it goes out, making it clear that the
He who is Immanent is the I that is resident!

The regulation and restrictions imposed on daily life
by the sages of India, the prescriptions for controlling and
directing impulses and attitudes that they recommended,
are all valuable in gredients of the culture and should be
treasured, and put into practice. The world is the triple
complex of *gunas* (attributes)---*Saathwik, Raajasik* and
Thaamasik (the balanced, the passionate and the dull).

The *Upanishadhs* say the that thunder teaches a
three-fold lesson, *dha dha* and *dha--dhaya, dhama* and
dharma---to the persons entangled in these three *gunas*.
Dhama (self-control) to the *Saathwik* who craves for
Aanandha (bliss); *dharma* (right conduct, ideals of
righteousness) to the *Raajasik*, who craves for adventure,
heroism and activity; and *dhaya* (compassion, based on
Love, which enables attachment and sublimates greed) to
those dominated by the *Thaamasik* qualities like craving
for objective pleasures through attachment to senses.

The sages discovered the truth '*Thath Thwam Asi*' ('That Thou Art'). '*That*' is the Divine, out of which all *this* arose, of which all *this* is, into which all *this* merges. It can be known by the *Bhakthi maarga*—the path of dedication, of devotion and surrender of the Self. The '*thou,*' that is to say, the Individual can be understood by the *Karma maarga*—the path of selfless activity, of the abnegation of the consequences of all activity, done in a spirit of adoration and with as much sincerity as an act of worship. Then, the process of identification of *Thath* and *Thwam* (That and Thou) called the recognition of the *Asi* has to be consummated, through *Jnaana maarga*—the path of knowledge, of sharp and relentless discrimination. When *Bhakthi* and *Karma* merge, it leads to *Jnaana. Bhakthi* sees everything as *Thath*; *Karma* wipes out the separateness of the *Thwam*. So, the *Asi* (identification) process becomes easy.

Rendering services to the poor effaces the ego

Though all this is simple and explained in various texts that are expounded by eminent teachers everyday to thousands, the truth is not experienced, the identity is not tasted. It is all stage acting. The words are not from the heart; they follow the cue of the script, written by another person. More is done for effect on the audience, and for the sake of applause and the yield at the counters! Of what benefit is heavy shower of rain, if you keep your buckets, upside down? Can it collect any water? When you listen to discourses on religion, if your minds are not receptive, you derive no benefit therefrom, do you?

Dr. Mistry spoke about the *Seva dhal* activities in Bombay; about the donation of blood, about their visits to the hospital wards and rendering services to the poor inpatients. Really, this is work that effaces the ego and endows one with real *Aanandha*. Dr. Mistry is Parsi; note how he has mastered the Hindu scriptures also, so that he explained now to you how Shiva, Paarvathi and Ganapathi can be interpreted as symbols of the *Karma, Bhakthi* and *Jnaana maarga* to the Goal.

Seva rendered in the faith that all are Forms of the One God is the highest *Karma.* You must watch and see that the inspiration for the *Seva* comes from the heart, not the head. When I was speaking some time ago to the Lecturers and students of the Arts and Science College at Whitefield, I told them of the need to revere elders. The students now greet teachers with a nod, a movement of the head, that is all. I told them that the nod meant distance, hostility, discord. It makes it clear that students and teachers are engaged in opposite camps, that they are strangers. I wanted them to give up such ideas, accept teachers as friends, guides engaged in their *Seva* while themselves students. I wanted love and reverence to flow back and forth between the two.

Heroic exploits of Krishna and Balaraama

I must now finish and go to the children of the *Vedhapaathashaala,* (School of *Vedhic* Studies) in the green room. They will enact a play saturated with spiritual nectar. For, God is described by those who have tasted Him, *"Raso vai sah"* (He is nectar itself)! His story is bound to be sweet beyond words. The universe is sweet on account of Him; it gives joy because it is He. You do not know how to grasp that joy and hold on to it; so, you swing between joy and grief. Acquire it to the full and for all time; then, there is no birth, no death. You are immortal, you are Bliss, Power, Wisdom.

In this play, about to be acted by the boys, I depict the incidents in the lives of my old *Bhakthas,* Kamsa, the Gopees, Akrura, Devaki, Vasudheva and Nandha. It is the good fortune of these boys that I was with them, many evenings, singing and repeating the lines, so that they may learn these great truths, enact the inspiring events before you and both derive and distribute joy. The boys may not be able to represent the roles to the fullest, but, yet you can imbibe the ecstasy and the spiritual lessons it in intended to convey.

The story starts with Kamsa plotting to bring his arch-enemy(!) Krishna, the seven-year-old cowherd boy, with his brother Balaraama into his city and palace, so that he could kill him, with the help of either the royal elephant, or the royal wrestlers. The subsequent scenes depict the agony of the maids of Gokul at the separation from the Divine Boy, the dilemma that agitates the foster-parents, and the departure of the Brothers to Mathura, where Kamsa was awaiting them. Krishna accepts the hospitality of an indigent devotee, rather than that of the monarch who had invited him; his arrival causes great joy to the populace. Meanwhile, his parents who are in jail are elated at the prospect of seeing him, after years of separation. The warders inform them, as and when it happens, the series of triumphs that the City resounds with, marking the heroic exploits of Krishna and his brother, the killing of the elephant, of the wrestlers and finally of the humiliation and destruction of the King, Kamsa himself! Krishna and Balaraama enter the jail and liberate the parents, and there the play ends.

Do not attach importance to the tender age *of the actors; the words emanating from them are wise and curative; they are the teachings of the Vedhas* and *Shaasthras.* Treasure them in your hearts and depart to your places determined to put at least a few into daily practice.

Prashaanthi Nilayam, 17.10.1969

26. Soldiers and Generals

GOD has given you this great chance, this wonderful world to be used as a gymnasium for the development of mental peace, and as a mint to transmute your base metal into valuable currency. You should therefore offer gratitude to Him for the shower of Grace. Even insects have this sense of gratefulness! An ant was caught on a dry leaf that was being carried down a flooded river and it called out from its tiny heart to God for succour. God prompted a kite that was flying over the river to dive and rise up, with the leaf on its beak; for He made the bird mistake it for a fish or frog! The bird was sorely disappointed, but, the ant was delighted to land on hard ground! God came as a kite and rescued me, it felt. I must be grateful to the bird, to all birds, it resolved. One day, while on its morning round, it saw a hunter aim an arrow at a bird; it bit the heel of the hunter, just when he was releasing the mortal shaft; the aim failed; the bird flew off, and was saved. The ant had paid its debt.

Man too has to pay his debts. He is heavily indebted to God for all the good, the true and the beautiful, with which he is endowed. He must pay the debt he incurs when he hears a discourse; this is done by ruminating over what has been told and practising at least a few of the ways of life that have been recommended. The meal that is eaten has to be digested, so that it may strengthen the bloodstream and transform itself into courage, skill and stamina. The world into which he is born has to be watched and studied with care and discrimination; the word, 'world,' means all that is not I, everything that the I calls mine: body, senses, mind, intelligence.

Spirituality cannot thrive in loveless hearts

God is everywhere, He is everything; so, it appears as if He is nowhere, and He is not in anything! For, to know Him you have to identify Him as someone foreign and something unique. We forget that everything is foreign to us, everything has a uniqueness of its own! On what authority can you deny? On what authority do you accept? You cannot deny Love, or Truth or Wisdom. He is Love, Power, Truth, Wisdom, Beauty. When you accept Love, you accept God. The tender plant of spirituality can grow only in the field of Love. It cannot thrive in the dehydrated loveless land of human hearts.

Remove all traces of salinity from your hearts adding to the soil the precious complement of the Name of the Lord. Water it with Faith. Then plant the seedlings of Divinity; have discipline as the fence, and steadfastness as the pesticide to be sprayed. Then, you can reap the rich harvest of *Jnaana*, which will free you from the task of cultivation for ever. Those who laugh at people doing *Bhajan* or visiting temples or attending Divine discourses have not tasted the nectar, and are therefore,

prejudiced against it. Pity them, for they do not know
what they miss.

But, these people do help the aspirant, by hindering
his aspiration! People pray to me, "Baaba! Put an end to
the machinations of these unbelievers!" But I know how
useful these traducers are. When the millet has grown to
a certain height, you can see the ryot taking a prong and
digging the soil, all round the stem; you may fear that he
is damaging the plant by hurting its roots. No, that
operation only helps to make that plant grow better, and
sturdier! Certain fruit trees too have to be pruned often!
Opposition, criticism, even downright condemnation are
necessary to confirm, consolidate and promote real faith.
The tests only deepen the conviction. What is the good in
having a nose that falls off at the first sneeze?

Yearn to see the resident in the Body

Some call on God only for help in distress. As the
Thelugu saying goes, "*Sankatam vasthe, Venkataramana!*"
(When suffering comes, you call on God Venkataramana!)
Until recently, pilgrims who climbed the series of steps that
lead them up the seven hills to the shrine of
Venkataramana, used to shout 'Govindha! Govindha!' so
that their legs may not ache; now, roads are laid right up
to the temple door, and cars and buses take pilgrims
straight to the very Presence! So, the only ache people have
nowadays is ache in the stomach, due to overeating and
want of exercise!

How will God reveal Himself when the seeker rides
to His Presence smooth in a swell car, and sticks to his
regular routine of luxury? Yearn to see the resident in
the temple of your body, do not yearn for keeping the
body safe, trim and coddled, in costly comfort. There are
some ultra-modern *Saadhakas*(!) who do not want to

cross their thresholds, or spend a paisa, or move a muscle, but, who yet demand that Self-realisation must drop lightly on their laps, from the *Guru* or from God, whom he should be able to persuade or manipulate! And, there are *Gurus* who cater to such(!) so that they can collect a pile!

You may complain that God is hard and heartless, since He does not respond to prayer, give signs from His pictures, speak from 'nowhere' in clear unambiguous terms, assuaging, assuring, advising---but, let Me tell you, God is Love; Love is God. His *Aakara* (Form) is *Prema* (Love); His *swabhauva* (essential nature) is *Aanandha* (Bliss); His *Raktha* (life-blood) is *Sathyam* (Truth). When even the stony cliff echoes your voice and responds when you cry, will not the softest, sweetest, love-filled heart of God respond? When there is no response, infer that there is something wanting in the cry. Perhaps the cry is hollow, insincere, mere play acting, set to a pattern, addressed to some one alien to oneself, taken to be far away and distant, as a tyrant or taskmaster.

Ignore trivial matters for the larger interests

Know that God is the One that is dearest and nearest to you, as dear and as near as your own heart and pray to Him; surely, His answer will be vouchsafed immediately. A hundred such individuals will leaven the whole earth. You may have huge hordes of men in the army, but they are useful only when the few generals who lead them know where they are and whether they should proceed, and how overcome the enemy, whose strength and weakness they have comprehended. Hordes of people sing, recite, adore, worship, praise, prostrate---but, these are the soldiers. Those who believe, who have faith and who practise the discipline, these are the Generals in whom the Master confides.

The future of this holy land lies with few who practise spiritual disciplines and set an example to others of the bliss one can acquire by those means. They alone can establish *Prashaanthi* and destroy *Ashaanthi* (anxiety and restlessness). I harp, day after day, on the need to practise steady faith and discipline. This may be irksome for some of you. Sometimes I feel I have spoken enough, that it is time I gave you some rest. But, soon, that resolution is overcome by compassion! And I am here, addressing you again! My belief is that, as the music master says, You master the melody by constant effort to reproduce it, not otherwise. In the corner of a few hearts at least a portion of what I advise may get stuck and from thence, it is bound to transform the daily lives, attitudes and emotions of the persons so affected.

When the rains pour, many feel miserable; they complain of bad weather, of not being able to move about! But, consider the lasting benefits that rains confer! We had good rains during the last three days. Some people told me, "Swaami! Why don't you will that rains should not disturb the even tenor of the activities here?" Well, these are trivial matters, for which the larger interests should not be set aside. As a matter of fact, the *Yajna* that was celebrated is to persuade the Gods to shower rains! And, it has succeeded in that aim! Rains promote harvests and prosperity. The *Yajna* is done here by the priests in strict conformity with *Vedhic* injunctions and so, even while the rite is on, the winds gather clouds of rain!

Prashaanthi Nilayam, 18.10.1969

27. The true time-table

CAUGHT in the coils of the 'created,' man is blind to the fact that he is part of the Divine Creator; identifying himself with the physical sheath in which he is encased, he is blind to the unity of all beings in the One Universal Absolute. Man has written and studied countless texts on spiritual discipline and discovery, and confounded the confusion, indulging in dialectical rivalries and argumentation. But, he who has put at least a page or two of these tomes into practise, is rendered silent, innocent of any desire for fame or victory. He is happy in the depths of his being. He ploughs the inner field, sows the seeds of love and the plants yield the flowers of fortitude, which fructify as *Shaanthi* (Equanimity). This is the message of the *rishis* of this land.

Each human being has three errors to correct: *mala* (dirt, filth), *vikshepa* (distraction) and *aavarana* (con-cealing; covering-up). *Mala* is the basic *ajnaana* (ignorance), which makes the tenth man (who counts the other nine and does not know that he is the tenth) declare that there is no tenth man. This *ajnaana* or *mala* is the miasma that causes the declaration, *aavarana*. And, *vikshepa* is the effect of that ignorance which makes all the ten search in the river for the lost man. *Mala* is the consequence of *karma*, in this and in previous lives. This can be removed by *nishkaamakarma* (activity with no attachment to the consequent benefit or loss). The *aavarana* effect can be overcome, by the cultivation of *sahana* (tolerance) and *anyonyatha* (feeling of belonging to one another). If only the ten were bound together by mutual solidarity no one would have been taken as missing! So too, *vikshepa* can be conquered by *prema* (love). Love would have revealed each to the other, and no one would have been 'missed.' This is the way to equip yourself with *Aanandha* (bliss Supreme)—the way of love, dedication and service.

Never use expressions which sear and hurt

There are some other things you can do to lead you to the consummation. For example, adhere strictly to truth. *Manah sathyena shuddhya the*---the mind is cleansed by Truth. Truth is the great purifier. It admits no dirt or sin, no defect or deceit. Falsehood pollutes the tongue of the speaker, the ear of the listener and the air which carries it from tongue to tympanum. There are beneficent and malificent sounds, and they produce corresponding echoes in the atmosphere. Words that emanate from faith in God and the humility it fosters will render the atmosphere pure, while those trumpeted by vanity and execrated by nihilism and atheism will contaminate it.

Use only such sounds as will cleanse the air. Do not be harsh; never use expressions which sear and hurt, which are the evil progeny of hate and pride. Praise the Lord, recite His Glory---that is the duty you owe yourself and others. The *raison d'etre* for this *yaaga* is just this; every sound of the *Vedha* is in praise of God and when the *Vedha* is recited with the proper cadence, exactly as prescribed in the traditional schools, the atmosphere will certainly undergo a remarkable transformation, and the men who breathe it will be a little less evil thereafter. Faith in God will instil faith in themselves and in others, and the world will be happier thereby. The Americans might walk on the moon, or the Russians picnic on the planet Mars, but, they have both to return to Earth, which is their common home.

You know from the *Raamaayana* that the severed head of Raama was once presented before Seetha, to make her give up all hope of meeting him again; the *Raakshasas* (demons) displayed before Raama, in the same manner, the severed head of Seetha, in the hope of making him give up all hope of recovering her alive. Both these heads were dummies prepared to deceive; they were not genuine. So too, one can claim genuine victory only when one has reached not the dead satellite, but the living Star, not the *Chandhra* (Moon) but the Raamachandhra—the Lord who rules over the inner satellites, the inner planets, the inner motives and agitations.

The real time-table of activities for man

When one's inner reactions and agitations are transmuted into Divine, all that one experiences through the senses, the mind and the intellect take on the Divine lustre, reveal their Divine core, and man is shaped in the mould of Love. One can be in the world but yet unaffected by it, provided this vision is gained. All activity will then be for the Almighty, by His Grace and through His Will. Do not get work done through cooks, servants, *aayahs*, and others, in the home; women must not depend on these, for the care of their children or attendance on their husbands.

Earning leisure for *Dhyaana* (meditation), through these servants, is not a spiritual gain. Do all the household work as acts of worship for Him; that is more fruitful than hours of *Dhyaana*, hours gained by entrusting this precious work to paid helpers. Men too must feel that frittering away precious time, flitting from one vanity to another and seeking more and more purposeless means of spending days and nights is detrimental to the main aim of life. Spread joy, give strength, distribute courage, console the distressed, help the lame to walk and the blind to see---that is the real time-table of activities of man. India has been reduced into a beggar-nation, since her children gave up these ideals and enthroned the ego, as the only God to be worshiped.

We are having here another All-India Conference of the Office-bearers of the Sathya Sai Organisations, so that these workers can once again remind themselves of this Message. When the petromax lamps become dim, we pump air in, and they become brighter. These lamps tend to burn dim and so we call them to this place for *Sathsang* and pump inspiration and instruction into them; their batteries get re-charged, for further service.

India has always stood forth on the side of virtuous character, maintained through vigilance, in perfect trim. Without that steady, strong character, achievements like scholarship or *siddhis* (skill in *yogic* powers) are like plastic fruits, deceptive imitations incapable of yielding joy. When the mind is engaged in the recital of God's Glory and the names of God, there can be no temptation to stray into the rake's highway of insane desire. Twice a day, morning and evening, if you spare some time to sing the names of God, with like-minded persons, all in unison, with full awareness of the deeper significance of each name as it sweetens the tongue, it will be of considerable help to establish the feeling of the constant presence of God, within you and without.

Prashaanthi Nilayam, 19-10-1969

28. The profound pastime

NOWADAYS, man has got into the habit of acting and talking as per his whims. There is no control exercised by conscience or moral sense or manners. For one who is so perverse, who is determined to go down to his doom, there in no need for counsel. Medicine is for the ill, not for the wholly healthy, or the wholly dead. Counsel is for those who suffer from doubt, anxiety or agitation. This counsel is contained in the *Shaasthras* and the sacred texts. A letter can be cast aside, once its contents have been noted, and the instructions communicated through it have been grasped. So too, these *Shaasthras* and texts are to be laid aside, once they are read, understood and followed. There is no purpose in reading them, over and over again.

The texts declare that you are not Ramiah or Kamiah or Bheemaiah---the name-labels you now parade as your own---but, you are really the *Aathma*, (the Being) the same that animates all Creation! Geetha teaches this very truth: he who knows this is "Arjuna," he who does not, is the blind King, "Dhritharaashtra!" *Dhritha* means, 'holding fast

to', and *raashtra* means 'the state'. The blind King held
fast to the state and refused to yield even five villages
to the rightful owners of half the kingdom! He was so
tenacious in his greed. He was attached to something
that was not 'he'; and that brought about his destruction.
Love everything as you love yourself; you cannot
possibly love them more than that! For, a vessel can
contain only its full. You cannot overfill it; you love
yourself best; that is to say, 'God,' who is your real self!

Deluded man allows thieves to become his masters

The guards at the gate have to be vigilant that thieves
do not gain entrance into the house, isn't it? The body of man
is a temple, where God is installed. The guards are *Shama*
and *Dhama*---the control of the senses and of the emotions.
If they are inefficient or idle, lust and greed, anger and envy,
hate and pride, sneak in, spread and hold sway over the
temple; man is so deluded that he honours these thieves, as
if they are the masters of the house they have stolen into! Be
master of your own mind. Be awake; arise and confront the
thieves, before they capture your treasure.

That treasure is the awareness of God in all. If there
were no thieves in the house, the master can utilise the
treasure to his own advantage but, when the thieves are
in, he is incapable of benefitting by his "kinship with
creation." He feels that he is the body, that he is distinct
and alone, that he is surrounded by friends and foes, and
afflicted by conspiracies to harm him. He does not love
others intensely: he suffers from fear or fondness.

The fundamental foolishness from which faults in
character and conduct emanate is the belief that what one
does is invariably right and just! This is the subtle effect of
the virus, EGO. A ryot was once bitten by a vicious dog,
owned by a merchant. In sheer self-defence he gave a blow

on its head, with the heavy stick he was carrying at the
time. The ferocious beast fell dead, and the irate merchant
took the ryot to the police station and filed a complaint
against him! Before the magistrate, the merchant argued
that the ryot could have hit somewhere else than on the
highly vulnerable head. It was his pet dog! But, the ryot
replied, "The dog bit me with its teeth; if it had bitten me
with its tail, I could have hit its hind quarters!" Whatever
is to our advantage will appear right to us; we do not usually
look upon a matter from the other fellow's standpoint. This
leads to endless complications.

Each place has its peculiar vibrations

The food that one eats has to be pure, free from the subtle
evils radiated by the persons who collect the materials, who
cook the dishes and who serve them. Yes; all these have to
be carefully watched by the *saadhaka*. The place where one
spends his life has also subtle influence on character and
ideals. Raamakrishna Paramahamsa used to speak of the
peace that one could get in Mathura, Vaaranasi and other
holy places. Though the Ganga is a river that is holy every
yard of its long journey to the sea, some spots on the banks,
like Rishikesh, Haridhwaar, Kaashi, Prayaag, etc., are
specially surcharged with spiritual vibrations that help the
saadhaka to cleanse his consciousness, in all its levels.

Each place has its peculiar vibrations, which affect the
occupant. A noted dacoit had built for himself a hide-out in
the remote recess of a jungle; two persons, a man and wife,
caught in terrible rain, took shelter therein; they were not
affected much by the waves of cruel greed, with which the
atmosphere in the hut was contaminated. But, when, after
few minutes, a monk walking through the forest ran in
and sought refuge from the rain, his immaculate heart
quickly got blackened! The clean mind quickly caught the

clot. The monk discovered himself contemplating the
murder of the couple and robbing them of the jewels they
wore. So that he may rebuild his hermitage richly to
teach *Yoga*, to all the world. He got so ashamed of himself
that he ran out again into the rain and saved himself
from perdition!

This is the *raison d'etre* for the insistence on *sathsang*
(good company), pious comradeship for spiritual aspirants.
The pious will be unselfish, not self-seeking. They are their
own best friends and the friends of others. When you are
in *sathsang*, your ears have a filter---you will hear only
things that are benignant, never anything malignant! Like
a rain-heavy cloud, they come down among the low and the
weak, to pour joy and courage. Like a fruit-laden branch,
they bend within reach of the hungry.

A poet's role is sovereign in the human community

This evening, we heard a number of poets recite their
compositions. The poet is known as *kavi*, a word pregnant
with supreme value in our ancient language, Sanskrit.
Kavim puraanam anushaasithaaram---the *kavi* (seer-
poet) is 'timeless'; he is the maker of laws for human
progress. He has, by means of his heightened intuitive
faculty, realised the beginningless and endless expanse of
Time; he has experienced the God dwelling within him
and others; he knows the Object, the Mirror and the
Image. It is indeed a sovereign role, the role of the true
poet in the human community.

Poets who barter their talents for a paltry purse, or for
cheap fame, are rhymsters, and very often not even that!
They start praising patrons and donors, who fling them
crumbs from their tables---a few *idlies* or a cup of coffee!
Such men are poltroons, and a blot on society. Poets must
have elevated ideals; they must charge themselves with

an enthusiastic love for the culture of the people; they must see the handiwork of God, the greatest Poet of all, in every grain of dust, in every twinkle of light, in every drop of rain, in every whiff of air. Their inner joy must surge over along the path of peace to bliss. Poetry has to be honey in the ear and balm on the heart.

The poems of the past had these qualities, and so, they are eternal, in their inspiration. They deal with the fundamental and eternal thirst of man and they are rich in thirst-quenching nectar. They satisfy and build up strength. Without spiritual *saadhana*, the expansion of one's consciousness, the broadening of one's sympathy, the deepening of one's contact with oneself as seen in and through all others, poetry is but a purposeless pastime.

Cultivate equanimity and equal vision before you embark on poetry.

Dashara, Prashaanthi Nilayam, 20-10-1969

Remembrance of the Lord's Name is the best detergent for the mind. It is the means of crossing the sea. The name is the raft that will take you safely across. The name will remove the veil of illusion, that now hides the Universal from the Individual. When that veil fades out, man finds Himself before himself; he beholds the Universe that he is.

Sathya Sai Baaba

---

29. Win the one

$\mathbf{B}$HAARATHEEYAS have a way of laying down do's and don'ts for every activity, for each part of one's duty to oneself and others; they are amenable to discipline, and self-control, because they know the joy that can be derived from limitations and restrictions. They are also eager to 'experience' rather than 'expound' spiritual truth; the emphasis from the very beginning of the *Vedhic* Age has been on 'how much have you earned' rather than on 'how much have you learned.' They know that the final beatitude is something inexplicable, that there are certain stages beyond the senses, the intellect, the emotions, and even beyond the ego, and that these stages confer the utmost ecstasy.

The sages have laid down three categories which comprise the knowable world: God, Nature and the I. (*Ishwara, Prakrithi* and *Jeeva*). God when seen through the mirror of Nature appears as I. Remove the mirror; there is only God; the image merges in the Original. Man is but the image of God. Even Nature is but an appearance of God; the Reality is He alone. The principle of appearance that deludes as multiple manifestations, is *maayaa*. It is not external to God; it is inherent in God, just as all powers are inherent in Him.

When the I image is conceived as distinct, we have dualism or *dhwaitham*. When it is recognised as only an unreal image, but yet, when it is given some relevance as related to the Original, then it is *Visishtha-adhvai-tham* (Qualified Monism). When both the 'I' image and the mirror are recognised as illusions and dismissed as such, only One remains---this is the *Adhwaitha Darshanam* (the Vision of the One, without a Second). The search for the one, without a second, is the search of India, since ages. The endeavour has always been to discover the One, which when known, all else can be known. The knowledge that is worth while is the knowledge of Unity not Diversity. Diversity means doubt, dissension, dispiritedness. The seen is different from the seer; the seer in everyone is the same.

God is like Gold which subsists through all the jewels

There are four stages in *saadhana*: the first takes you to *Saalokya*: You are in the kingdom of God. You have to obey the King's commands, be loyal to him, respect his lightest wish and serve him sincerely, surrendering without any reservation. The next stage is *Saameepya*: It is the stage when you are in the palace as one of the couriers or courtiers or chamberlains or servants. You are nearer to Him, and develop Divine qualities. The next stage is *Saaroopya*: The *saadhaka* imbibes the Form of the Divine, that is to say, he is like the brother or near kinsman of the King, entitled to wear royal robes and para-phernalia. And lastly, we have the *Saayujya*, when as the Crown Prince, he succeeds to the throne and becomes Monarch himself. The subject is as the limb, the King is as the heart.

The mind that does not know the One is a dry leaf, rising with every gust of wind, and falling when it subsides. But, the mind fixed in the awareness of the One is like a rock, unaffected by doubt, stable, secure. God, as amenable to worship and contemplation, is referred to as *Hiranyagarbha*—Golden Womb, the Origin of Creation, the Immanent Principle that has willed to become manifest and multiple. The term Gold is appropriate, for gold is the One from which multifarious jewels are shaped by the craftsman, to suit the needs, fancy, foibles and fashions of wearers. God too is shaped by human imagination, inclination and intellect into various forms, grand or grotesque, frightening or charming. Man erects these images, and pours out before them, his fears, fancies, desires, dreads and dreams. He accepts them as masters, comrades, monarchs, teachers, as the moment dictates. But whatever man may do with God, God is unaffected. He is Gold, which subsists in and through all the jewels.

Renounce your identity with the body to realise God

He is in you, and it is He that has prompted you to project Him into the outer world, as this idol or that image, to listen to your outpouring and give you peace. Without the inspiration, solace, and joy that He confers from within, you will be raving mad, as one who has lost his moorings and is tossed about, rudderless on a stormy sea. Hold on to Him in the heart, hear Him whisper in the silent words of counsel and consolation. Hold converse with Him, guide your footsteps as He directs, and you reach the goal, safe and soon. The picture before which you sit, the flowers which you place on it, the hymns you recite, the vows you impose on yourselves, the vigils you go through---these are activities that cleanse, that remove obstacles in the way of your getting aware of the God within.

Really ... you are carryi... its own house, the ...u are He; not this body which body goes, the Light o... like the snail, loaded with illumine your thoughts, wo... the fascination for the in the Geetha that He will releas... ...ithin will shine and moment you renounce *Sarvadharma*—all ...eeds. Krishna says and responsibilities, of rights and duties, of ...om bondage, the me'; that is to say, He requires the renunciation of th... identity of the individual with the Body.

That is the *Dharma*, the Supreme Duty which Krishna had come to teach. Man has a duty to himself---recognising that he is Divine, and nothing else. When he neglects this, and strays into the bypaths, God incarnates and brings him on the right path again.

Fight against the six demons infesting your mind

The need comes first and then the teaching to suit the need, the form to impart the teaching. Naaradha, the Celestial Sage, is said to have suffered from mental agitation and the sage Sanathkumara taught him the *Vedhas*, to restore peace of mind. The *Vedhas* cannot therefore be said to be beginningless; there are many names of sages and 'poets' mentioned in the *Vedhic* Hymns and so, the hymns are subsequent to the birth of those persons.

Vaalmeeki is said to have composed the *Raamaayana* and taught it first to the twin children of Raama, who later sang the whole epic before the Divine Hero, their father, in open Durbar (King's Court). When you emphasise the container, the body, the bulb, and not the contained, the soul, the current, then, you talk of this God and that, of the Creator Brahma, the Protector Vishnu, the Destroyer Shiva! But, really, this body and the bodies in front of

Me are all the same, only ... current in each
is different, though the ... the same.
The six demons—... (lust), *krodha* (anger), *lobha*
(greed), *moha* (... ...ent), *madha* (pride) and
maathsarya (... pursue you and turn you into wrong
paths and ...you servile, stupid and sad. Fight
against th... resolutely. That is the life-long war you
have to wage. It is not a Seven Years War, or a Thirty
Years War, it may be a Hundred Years War, if you live
a hundred years. The struggle knows no respite! This is
a civil war, where vigilance alone can bring dividends.
Arjuna prayed to Krishna, "The mind is infested by these
demons; it does not afford me a moment of rest." Krishna
said, "Give it to me!" Easy, is it not? Like the bee which
hums until it reaches a flower and starts drinking the
nectar, the mind too will clamour, until it settles on the
Lotus Feet of the Lord, and then, it is silent, for it is engaged
in tasting Divine Nectar! Once it discovers the nectar, it
will not flutter any more.

Sages guided the monarchs of ancient kingdom

Dedicate yourself to God. Sudhaama was asked by
the Lord, "Tell me what you need!" He replied, "I need
you and you alone," for, that includes all! The little son
asks the father for a book, a bush-shirt, a ball, and a pen.
If only he wins the love of the father, he has no need
even to think of the items that he requires. The father
will anticipate his needs and provide the articles.

This consideration goaded the monarchs in the
ancient kingdoms of India to seek counsel from some
sage, who had no affiliations and prejudices, who
therefore knew what best to do, in any crisis. They
were men full of love for humanity, compassion for the
distressed, and understanding of the motives of the

wrong-doers. They were of five grades of spiritual greatnes. *Pandiths, Rishis, Raajarishis, Maharishis* and *Brahmarishis*. They were free from any trace of ambition, or avarice to amass land, wealth or fame. Sage Vasishta, the Preceptor and Counsellor of Emperor Dasharatha, initiated Raama into the mystic formula, called *Aadhithyahridhaya*, the 'Heart of the Sun,' directing him to recite it whenever victory appeared to slip out his grasp! These counsellors steered the kingdom safe. A rain was needed to put down the conflagration lit by the wicked cousins, which was fed by oil (Karna) and wind (Sakuni), and so, Krishna arranged for a Rain of Arrows, at Kurukshethra.

If the ruler bases his rule on the faith that God resides in all, and that every individual is to be respected as such, then there will be no discontent or discord. That is the *Vedhaanthic* foundation on which aspects of living have to be built. The Buddha too built his religion on the *Vedhaantha*, though he might not have acknowledged the source; the Source was something taken for granted, it was never disputed. It was inescapable.

The spiritual alone give happiness and joy

The spiritual alone can confer happiness, can give lasting fame and joy. For example, years ago, the atmosphere of India was echoing with the fame of three patriots, Laal, Baal and Paal. Of these, the name of Baal Gangadhar Thilak may last longer than those of Laala Lajpathrai or of Bipin Chandra Paal, for, Thilak wrote the *Geetharahasya*, a commentary on the Bhagvadgeetha. Your bodies have been acquired for realising God, and dedicating them for searching the Divine, serving the Divine and sustaining the Divine---that alone can satisfy your innermost craving and remove the gnawing discontent.

Prashaanthi Nilayam, 21.10.1969

30. Beauty and duty

YOUR task as *swayam sevaks* (self-servants) will be done, when you know full well the task for which you have earned this human frame, with all its potentialities and possibilities. It is to grow in love, expand that love, practise love, strengthen love and finally become Love and merge in the Illimitable Love, which is God. All your life, you must be Love, with Love, for Love. That is to say, love expressed through service to those that draw that love from you, and by drawing, help to increase it and deepen it. Spiritual discipline is designed to canalise that love, so that it may irrigate the heart, which will otherwise go dry.

The volunteers privileged to work at the Prashaanthi Nilayam have to set the ideal for similar workers all over the world. For, here, service emanates from genuine understanding of the meaning and purpose of life. When that is known, every step will be right, towards righteousness. And, if there be righteousness in the heart, there will be beauty in the character; if there is beauty in the character, there will be harmony in the home; if there be harmony in the

home, there will be order in the nation; if there be ord
in the nation, there will be peace in the world. Righteousness consists in widening the horizon of your compassion.
This will necessarily promote the sum of human happiness.

Religion is three-fourths character. No person can
claim to be religious if he merely observes the sacraments
and rules, and fails to be upright and compassionate.
Character alone can harden one to the blows of pain and
pleasure. It alone can make man exclaim. "Death for me is
a joke; birth cannot make me afraid!" This week that you
have spent as volunteers here is a week of character-building
of *saadhana*. *Swayam* means self; *sevak* means servant. You
have been serving your own selves all these days.

Serve all as embodiments of the Divine Will

Continue in this state of mind, when you go back to
your villages and occupations. Do not give up your gains
and run after losing concerns. Serve all, as embodiments
of the Divine Will. That will give you immense joy, a joy
that no other activity can confer. The chakora bird waits
with open beak for the first drops of the very first rain that
comes from the sky; it relishes no other. So too, you should
yearn for the chance to console, comfort, encourage, heal,
help some one looking for it. See yourself in him; feel his
pain to be yours, his sorrow to be yours.

Of what profit is it to have a car, if you are ignorant of
the art of driving it or using it for moving about? Of what
profit is to have a radio, if you are unaware of its working
and of the ways of benefitting by it. Of what benefit is it to
have a body, if you do not seek to know how best to utilise it?
Learn from the saints and sages who have realised the Truth
about the path you shall tread and the goal you have to attain.
That Goal is God. He is beyond all notions of good and bad,
right and wrong. These are earthly measures, by which the

emporary is weighed and judged. He has no form, no limbs, no dualities, no preferences, no prejudices, no predilections. To say that He is *Sathyaswaruupa*, (having the characteristic of Truth), *Jnaanaswaruupa* (having full wisdom) and *Aanandhaswaruupa* (full of Bliss) is also not correct. For, He has no *Swaruupa* or *Swabhaava* (individual form or individual nature); He is *Sathya*; He is *Jnaana*; He is *Aanandha*. That is the experience of those who have tasted.

There are no pots, in the clay; but, in the pots, there is clay. So also there are no characteristics in God; but, in the characteristics of *Sathya, Jnaana* and *Aanandha*, there is God. God is everywhere, but, no spaceship can hit against Him, no space pilot can espy Him. He is too subtle for all that type of contact, subtler than ether (*Aakaasa*). So, do not lend your ears to people who swear there is no God. God is too vast, too far above the reach of reason or imagination. You can only get glimpses of the Bliss derivable from the contemplation of His Magnificence.

Prashaanthi Nilayam, 28-10-1969

Discriminate before you develop attachment. If you have attachment towards wife and children, land and buildings, bank accounts and balances and when these decline, you will come to grief. Develop attachment towards the Universal and you too will grow in love and splendour.

Sathya Sai Baaba

31. The colleges we need

THIS day marks a significant and sacred stage in the history of Ananthapur. It is also a great day for those who yearn for the revival and growth of *Bhaaratheeya* culture. The people of India are now giving themselves, through their Government, vast opportunities for the development of education, and of medical facilities, and the promotion of schemes for the provision of vaster quantities of foodgrains and drinking water. These will raise the standard of living of the millions; more houses are built; more schools, more hospitals, more factories, better farms, more trade---these are being planned and established. This is all desirable, no doubt. But, along with these, and even more than these, plans have to be devised and executed for guaranteeing for the millions security, contentment, equanimity and peace. These are inner accomplishments which will ensure a stable, satisfied community, which can embody the real culture of India and reveal its strength-giving qualities.

It is indeed surprising that neither the rulers nor the ruled have yet tried to diagnose the prevalent discontent, the recurrent waves of hate and misunderstanding that disturb the peace, the anxiety and fear that undermine social peace. The causes for these maladies are to be sought in the realm of the spirit, rather than in the economic, political or intellectual, scholastic or social fields. It is indeed deplorable that the education of the spirit has been totally neglected, while attention is devoted to the training of skills and to gleaning and garnering information.

Sahana gives peace, removes hatred

This College and other such colleges which I am establishing in every State of India has as one of its purposes, the demonstration to the people and the Administration, the urgency of this task as well as the ways in which it can be fulfilled. My Sankalpa (plan of action) is to provide the youth with an education which, while cultivating their intelligence, will also purify their impulses and emotions and equip them with the physical and mental disciplines needed for drawing upon the springs of calmness and joy that lie in their own hearts. Their higher natures will have to be fostered and encouraged to blossom, by means of study, prayer and saadhana, contacts with the sages, saints and spiritual heroes and heroines of their land, and place them on the path of self-confidence, self-satisfaction, self-sacrifice and self-knowledge.

The heart of man which is now allowed to lie fallow has to be ploughed by spiritual exercise like japam (repetition of sacred word) and dhyaanam (meditation) and naamasmarana (Chanting Lord's Name); then, when the seeds of prema are sown and fertilised by shraddha, and the crop protected by Thithiksha (vigilance), the harvest of sahana (endurance) can be gathered. Sahana gives shaanthi (peace), and removes hatred and anger. Sahana is the richest treasure of man.

To understand aright the culture of Bhaarath, people have to study the Puraanas (spiritual legends), which are the Pramaanas (authority) and the Shaasthras (spiritual sciences) which are the *Nethras* (eyes). Both these are designed to elaborate and simplify the profound teachings of *Vedhaantha*, and so, they can be called "popular manuals of spiritual science."

These *Puraanas* and *Shaasthras* stress the role of women as mothers and extol the mothers, who instilled high ideals in the minds of the children of the land. The *Vedhas* speak of Maithreyi and Gaargi, as great scholars and spiritual heroines. Gaargi was revered in the assembly of *Vedhic Pandiths* for her mastery of the abstruse problems of the spiritual voyage into the heights of self-realisation. In historical times, we have the mother of Shivaji who fed him on the epics and *Puraanas*, and brought him up as a brave representative of the best in Hindu Culture.

India should get back the status of *Guru* for mankind

Dharma for the Hindu, the adherent of *Sanaathana* Culture, is as near and as dear as his own body. To save it and sustain it, he was prepared to face exile, torture, death. *Dharma* was also the land whereon he lived, the breath wherewith he drew his vitality. He never cared to reside in a land where *Dharma* was not practised; he felt suffocated, when he had to be in an atmosphere that was polluted by *A-dharma* (life, contrary to the principles of *Dharma*). In the *A-dharmic* land, he can exist only as Seetha did in the Ashokavana of Lanka, breathing the ozone of *Raamanaama* and ignoring the entire environment.

Bhaarath can never find real happiness, except in the atmosphere of devotion and dedication to God; God is so much inter-twined in every word, act and thought of the people. Dams, factories, universities—these too will prosper, and attain the targets, only if the men and women involved in them and benefiting by them have the earnestness, the sincerity, the humanity and the reverence which *Bhakthi* (devotion) can build into them. It is only by this means that Bhaarath can, once again, attain the status of *Guru* (spiritual precept) which she had won and retained for centuries, the *Guru* for all mankind.

This college will be run by the Sathya Sai Trust, which has as advisers and associates a number of distinguished sons and daughters of India, full of the spirit of *yoga* (spiritual effort) and *thyaaga* (sacrifice) which are the distinct features of Bhaarath. They will foster the nobility of the Mother in our society and culture, and try to nourish in this institution the ideals which strengthen and support the educated, compassionate, cultured, loving, unselfish Mother, the Inspiration for the *Dharmic* (virtuous) life in this country.

The Trust does not look forward for any help, financially or otherwise from the citizens of Anantapur. It is satisfied when they derive *Aanandha*, watching the *Aanandha* of the Trust, its associates, the staff and the students of the college, the parents and the families of the students in the years to come. This college is not only for this town, but, it has to be a model and an eye-opener for all who are interested in the education of women and the uplift of our culture, through the mothers of the land. There is even a thought lurking in my mind to make Ananthapur the Centre of a University, perhaps a Women's University.

I desire that the relationship between citizens be founded more and more on Love, and that unity will establish itself more firmly, removing all traces of malice or envy or pride. Let the mind dwell more firmly on the universal *Aathma*, which is reflected equally in every being—and, Love will automatically guide all activities along fruitful paths. I bless that this college will be an example of the triumph that Love and Reverence can win. Let it be an inspiration to workers in the field of Women's Welfare and National Progress, in every State. May the college educate generations of noble mothers who will live *Dharma* and raise heroes surcharged with devotion and dedication to God.

Ananthapur: Foundation laying ceremony of the College by the Vice-President of India, 7-11-1969

32. The Three Thrones

THIS gathering of Office-bearers of the Sathya Sai Organisations from all over India fills all hearts with joy. This is a great occasion. Use this chance to re-discover and re-establish in your minds the high purpose to which this Organisation is dedicated; and to strengthen the faith that will inspire you to participate more fruitfully, in this epoch-making adventure. Organisational effort in the spiritual field has long been neglected in India; it is fraught with the danger of disruption through the subtle cankers of egoistic ambition and faction. Unless the individual is first purified and strengthened, the organisation will disintegrate and fall apart. Hence, it has all along been lone pilgrimages into the land of Light and Love. But, the very basis of spiritual progress is the denial of the I, and the joyful acceptance of the We, which is but the merging of the I in He. Sacrifice, service, sharing in the exaltation of others, compassion when others suffer grief---these are virtues that purify and prepare the individual to the arduous task of reaching the Goal. Expand the limited

awareness of the individual into the limitless realm of
Divine Glory—that has been the call, down the corridors of
Time.

Each unit is a limb of the *Swaaraajya* Organisation, no
doubt; a limb of the Organisation for Self-mastery, but, one
has to master the self so that he may be more fit for serving
man. This company of seekers must help each other, to
escape from the bondage of the senses and to live constantly
in the Presence of the Omni- present Lord, whom they have
contacted. The Unit is a perennial source of *Aanandha* for
the individual and the community. It is a lamp in the
wilderness; it uses the oil of devotion, the wick of service, and
sheds the light of Love through the flame of *Jnaana*. The
flame can be clean and smokeless, only when the person is
straight, sincere—revering others too as embodiments of
sincerity and straightforwardness, of Divinity itself.

Live along the guidelines set by the sages

At the present time, when people meet, a curtain of envy,
pride and misunderstanding intervenes between them,
exaggerating the foibles of each into obstacles in the path of
sympathy and brotherliness. They miss the basic unity, the
essential fraternity, the fundamental equality. Understand
and tolerate, sympathise and love—this is the message of the
sages of this land, who shaped and sustained the *Sanaathana
Dharma* (the Eternal Universal Religion). As Office-bearers
of the Units of this worldsaving Organisation, you have to
revive this Message, revitalise it and guide men, with your
experience. If you live along the guidelines of those sages, you
will make three people happy—you, him and Me!

Dedication detests publicity and pomp. It is a wedding
of the spirit with its Master. It is a treasure that is counted
in solitude. The sages knew how to conserve it and
contemplate on it, in blissful loneliness, deep in the recesses

of jungle hermitages. The soul was their sole companion and God the only counsellor. They wrestled with their inner foes, the temptations of the tawdry objective world; they put down doubts and diversions. Achieving the goal of perfect calm, people like Shankaraachaarya came and taught how to pray, propitiate and pass into the boundless.

The world is planned as a gymnasium

They taught by example that the most precious jewel in the human breast is Love---Love that sees all as Oneself. Now, it is locked safe in the chest that is chiselled out of the Five Elements, and its light is now shed only on the ego or those that cater to it. In reality, it is the heritage of all mankind and has to be shared with all. The world is planned as a gymnasium, a playground, a *thapovan* (hermitage) where man spends his days recouping his health and strength, earning clarity and purity of intellect; but, it has now become a *jinn-asium*, a slay-ground, a *thamo-van* (garden of sloth), reducing man into something worse than brute. Anger, hate, and pageantry have replaced love, cordiality and simplicity.

Devotion is not an acquisition to be advertised; it is a secret gain which has to be communicated only to God. When the spark of envy envelops the mind, it soon develops into a huge fire and destroys all chances of good. Watch for it vigilantly; envy is only the consequence of pride and pride comes of ignorance of your role. You believe that you have achieved much and that others are not giving you the respect due to you. They honour some one with less achievement, more than they honour you. But, just think for a while: Who granted you the chance, the intelligence, the success? The Lord. You are helpless without Him. He chose, He prompted, He executed, it was done. Be humble, be cordial with all. They are equally devoted and sincere.

Do not infect these Associations of Aspirants for My Grace with the virus of rivalry and factions. Do not inquire into the caste affiliations of any one and develop partiality or prejudice thereon. Strive to win the gift of My Grace, not the glitter of Presidentship or Secretaryship. Pay attention to your duties and responsibilities. This is no ordinary burden that you have been privileged to carry. I can see you through and through. Do not carry your head high, and taunt people. Stoop, so that you can pick your burden up and place it on the shoulders. Bend as the branch bends, it is heavy with fruit! Each duty well done is a deposit to your credit in the Bank of God! Fatten that deposit; you can draw on it by means of cheques; you can claim payment as of right.

You must have intense faith in the *Vedhas*, the *Shaasthras* and the *Puraanas*. They are the repositories of the ancient wisdom, the wisdom that has stood the test of ages. They teach humility, reverence and tolerance. Saturate yourselves with the spirit of those texts. Then, you will be free from the illnesses of sloth and covetousness, lust and gluttony, envy and pride. Enthrone Love as the Monarch of the Kingdom of Feeling! Enthrone Reason as the Monarch of the Kingdom of Thought! Enthrone Detachment as the Monarch of the Kingdom of Activity. This is the task I set for the Units of the Sathya Sai Organisation today.

Inauguration of All India Conference,
Prashaanthi Nilayam, 20-11-1969

Efforts to achieve health, comfort, etc., must be just enough for the purpose of sustaining the saadhana, not more, not less.   *- Sathya Sai Baaba*

33. The Hundredth and the next

THIS Conference where devotees from all the States of India have come together is a good opportunity to exchange ideas and chalk out programmes of activity. You can also present difficulties and doubts and return with faith strengthened and hesitation cured. You must keep politics away from the associations, for, these are exclusively for spiritual development. Where the rough and tumble of politics and party factions are prevalent, no spiritual discipline can flourish. You have to seek unity, love and peace, and not promote differences, debates and disputes. They belong to politics, that is to say, competition and contests for places of authority in the Units have corroded some associations even in this Organisation, because individuals have not learnt to control their ego, their minds have not been cleansed of *Raajasik* tendencies. *Dhaya, Dhama, Dhaana*---these are the three qualities that have to be cultivated by man. *Dhaya*: Compassion to curb the *Asuric* tendencies;

Dhama: Control to foster the *Daivic* qualities; *Dhaana* : Charity to hold in check the greed that is natural to man.

Ambition to earn fame in the world, to gain some position of authority over fellow-men, to lead luxurious life—this can never ensure *Shaanthi* (mental peace). Mental peace is the result of quite different attainments. Wealth cannot command it, nor authority commandeer it! It must be won the hard way, through meditation, *naamasmaran* and the nine steps to the Presence of the Almighty. It must be won on the earth, to which man rightfully belongs; and, not on any other heavenly body towards which he may dare navigate.

Know that *Thath* and *Thwam* are the same

You multiply grief by recollecting the past and picturing a lurid future. You fill the present moment with dread, recapitulating the past and reflecting on coming events! The needle runs over the gramaphone record and causes the music to play. The record is inert matter. When the mind (the needle) concerns itself with Nature, contacts Nature, the song of joy-grief is heard. The fault lies not in Nature, nor in the mind but in the contact! Keep aloof, be detached—then, there is no reaction at all. That is the path to earn mental peace.

The child has his tongue and the mother has hers. The mother keeps the child on her lap and pronounces the words so that the child may learn to speak. However busy the mother's tongue may be, the child has to speak through its own tongue. The mother cannot speak for the child and save herself all the bother! The *Guru* too is like that. He can only repeat, remind, inspire, instruct, persuade, plead; the activity, the disciple must himself initiate. He must jump over the stile himself. No one can hoist him over it!

Thath (That) is a word that refers to something in the distance. That, means something far away to which you point. *Thwam* (You) is yourself. It is the thing nearest to you, namely, you yourself. You know yourself most; what you have now to know is only this: that, "you" and "that," are the same! There is only One and no Two. It is spoken of as *'buddhi graahyam, atheendhriyam'*---graspable by the intelligence, beyond the grasp of the senses of touch, hearing, seeing, taste and smell!

The Lord Venkateshwara is celebrated as the Lord of the Seven Hills; His Temple is on the Seventh Hill and one has to traverse and go over six hills to reach Him. This is symbolic of the six obstacles of *Kaama* (Lust), *Krodha* (Anger), *Lobha* (Greed), *Moha* (Attachment), *Madha* (Pride) and *Maathsarya* (jealousy). One has to go across these passions and cast them behind him before he can stand face to face with the Lord.

In the petrified stratum called the body, dig with the help of the pickaxe called intelligence until you excavate the Diamond, *Jnaana*, from the soil, the Mind. Once you secure the precious stone, it matters not whether you wear it embossed in gold, namely, Nature (*Prakrithi*). Use *Prakrithi* to brighten or show off the Wisdom! That is harmless pastime. But, do not fall a victim to Nature as such; revere it only as the vesture of God.

Office-bearers cannot claim exemption or privilege

How can you climb the six hills and reach the seventh, if you hesitate even to ascend the first step? I laid down *Nagarasankeerthan* (group singing in the streets) as a spiritual discipline, even last year, at the World Conference at Bombay. But, today, at this Conference, I find the Sub-Committee recommends that Office-bearers must attend the *Nagarasankeerthan* at least six times in the year! Can you call this *Saadhana*? Office-bearers cannot claim any privilege or exemption. They must evince leadership; by their devotion and faith, they must inspire the waverers. That is their function.

But, now, they seek concessions! People crowd into film shows, rush towards social clubs, spend days together in playing cards---but, when they are asked to sing the Glory of God and purify themselves and the atmosphere, they clamour for concessions! When the heads hit against each other in anger, can the feet be steady and unaffected? They too will kick and trample as maliciously as they can. When the heads desire to opt out, the others too will lose enthusiasm and fade away. Realised souls, says the Geetha, act so that the world may be saved. While this is so, those eager to realise have to act, so that their progress may be unhampered.

I cannot accept the plea that people do not find time for going out on *Nagarasankeerthan*. If a hundred things can be done in the time now available, surely, the hundred and first thing can also be accommodated in the Time-Table. You can stop doing the hundred but this extra one is as the breath that sustains life itself. Do not join the group only when the cameraman is around; move with the party and feel the thrill. The Office-bearers must be one with the rest, in all the activities of the Unit. Be filled with joy that you have now got the lucky chance of listening to and carrying out the command! This chance comes rarely to man.

In Sai institutions minds must harmonise

When leaders shirk the tasks that they themselves have prescribed for the followers, even the strongest organisations suffer disintegration. Two trees rub against each other and a forest fire is the consequence; two stalwarts struggle for power and the institution is caught in conflagration! Do not enforce the rules, without mercy or thoughtful consideration. If a person does not attend 60 percent of the meetings, the rules say that he is to be removed from office. Give him chances to reform, to be within the group, so that he may reform. If even this does not mend, remove the name, without any compunction.

Do not have any one in, who would much rather be outside the group of *Sai Bhakthas*, either on account of his habits or indifference towards religious matters, especially towards the directions given by Me. For, My honour is your honour, your honour is My honour. This is not your Unit, your Organisation; it is Mine. In My institution, minds must mutually harmonise. The hearts of all have to be ploughed by discipline, and sowed with the seeds of Love, so that they grow into the Trees of Dedication, and yield the Fruits of *Jnaana*.

Office-bearers and Members of Sathya Sai Institutions must have *Sahana* (tolerance of opinions different from one's own), *Sathya* (Truth), *Dhaya* (Compassion) and *Prema* (Love towards all). They must revere their parents. They should not fall into the sin of preaching what they do not practise. Whoever neglects his parents, allows them to languish and suffer while he himself is enjoying a higher standard of life does not deserve to be a member, for I always stress the *Vedhic* injunction: *Maathru dhevo bhava* (consider mother as God), *Pithru devo bhava* (consider father as God). Those of you who are guilty of this malfeasance, take note, and be cured by this injunction. The Sathaya Sai Family must have only men and women, who honour their family obligation of nourishing and nursing their parents.

All India Conference, Prashaanthi Nilayam,
21-11-1969

34. *Doing the done*

INDULAL SHAH informed you about the resolutions adopted by the various sub-committees, suggesting modifications and additions to the rules already current, so far as the Organisation is concerned. The main purpose running through all these regulations is known to you; it is the establishment of *Sathsang* (Company of the pious), which will help the Realisation of the Reality, *Aathma-Saakshaathkaara*. It is to recover, in and through this agitated world, the peace that is your birthright, and utilise that peace for the illumination of the heart, which will reveal the splendour of the *Aathma* which you really are. So long as Arjuna believed that he was the doer and the enjoyer of the rewards for the deed, he was miserable. But, when the Lord taught him and demonstrated to him that he was but an instrument, that his duty was only to surrender to the Will of the Lord, that those whom he sought to kill had already been killed by the Lord, he was freed from grief; he was filled with unspeakable peace.

This is the teaching of all religions, a teaching that flows like a subterranean spring feeding all the external rites and ceremonies laid down in each religion according to the climate, geographic and demographic, of each region. These may be different from each other, but the basic lesson each religion teaches is to surrender to the sovereign Will of God, and leave the consequence of deeds well done, to the Lord Himself. It is His Will, and your only duty is to shape yourself into a fit instrument. To suppress the assertive ego, disciplines have been laid down in every religion, by every compiler of moral codes, by every educator and reformer of human morals. But the oldest, and most effective, and the most successfully practised system is the body of directives laid down in the *Vedhas* and *Shaasthras* of India.

Develop probing into the idea of 'I'

In a household, when the wife is a shrew, there can be no joy or peace. Or, if the husband is a drunkard and a cruel tyrant, the atmosphere is charged with hatred and grief. So too, in the body, when the mind is a shrew or when the intelligence is a tyrant, there can be no peace. The master of the household is the *Aathma* who is seldom recognised or identified as such. When the *Aathma* is discovered as the master, and recognised as such, joy reigns undisturbed in the home. Now, there is a certain 'I' used in speech and thought as possessing the body and the limbs, the senses and the mind and the reasoning faculty, but there is no attempt to probe into the idea of the 'I' and no keenness to spot out its whereabouts and characteristics. This is what is called *Aathma-vichaara* (deliberation on the Self); every unit must encourage its member to develop this *Aathma-vichaara* and not be content with the conventional items of club activity, like the unveiling of portraits. This search for the *Aathma* will be facilitated by a study of the

Upanishadhs and the Bhagavadgeetha, which is but the essence of *Upanishadhic* teachings.

Or, it is enough if *Prema* is cultivated, the *Prema* that knows no distinction between oneself and another, because all are but limbs of the One Corpus of God Almighty. Through Love alone can the Embodiment of Love be gained. Here, no scholarship is needed; in fact, scholarship will be an impediment, for it caters to egoism and it breeds doubts and the desire for disputation and laurel of victory over others preening themselves as learned! When this Love is established, no member of the Organisation will compete with another, or look down on another. The bond of love will knit all into a rare type of family, which knows only one Will and one direction. Malice extraordinary may persuade some low minds to resort to the courts of law, for paying off private scores, but no member of the Organisation will ever do so, in the administration of the units, who values the *Dharmasthaana* (abode of virtue) that is available in this Form and Name.

Do not fall a prey to the temptation of office

Since the Presidents, Vice-Presidents and Secretaries are the only persons invited for these Conferences, I find that each Unit is breaking up into two, so that some individuals who claim prominence can come. The person who went to court for an injunction against some one else attending this Conference had this in view! He wanted to deprive another of what he thought was a unique honour. I ascribe this to the perversion of mind due to greed for prestige. I do not ration Grace on these silly principles; a person may not hold any office, but he is entitled to Grace, provided he is sincere in the faith and steady in Love. Do not fall a prey to the temptation of office and position of authority in these *Samithis* and *Mandalis*. Hold the offices in rotation, so that all may get the opportunity of leading in service. There are some *Mandalis* and *Samithis* which select office-bearers by lot. The members feel that any one who is allotted the post is as good as the others.

The date for the beginning of the official year of the *Samithis* and *Sanghas* and *Mahilaasathsangs* and other units of the Organisations shall hereafter be the *Uttha-raayana Punyakaala, viz., the Makara Sankraanthi*, which usually falls about January 14th. Annual Reports should reach the District and State Presidents and the Headquarters soon after this date, along with the names of newly elected Committees, if any.

Another point to be noted is that public meetings can be arranged in a town or city only under the auspices of the *Samithi*. There should not be any competition between the *Samithi* and an over-enthusiastic subsidiary unit, in arranging public meetings, involving printing and distribution of invitations, reception of speakers, and elaborate expenses, preparations for seating, loud- speakers, etc. The units of the *Samithi* will not have the resources for such functions and if each unit seeks to outshine the others, the atmosphere of cordiality and co-operation will be fouled. There should not be any factional struggles between the members of any unit or between one unit and another.

Guidelines for conducting *Nagarasankeerthan*

About this *Nagarasankeerthan*: Do not start too early or too late; you must go through the streets slowly, singing aloud the Names of all manifestations, just when the people of the locality are awaking and preparing to meet the new day that is dawning. Do not carry any photo or picture with you, demonstrating your loyalty to any particular Form or Name. Walk along, in well arranged groups, men and women separately; do not plan *Nagarasankeerthan* in

buses, tractors, cycles or carts. Do not compete with each
other in singing *Naamaavalis* and cultivate envy or
hatred. Let those with a good voice and musical talent
lead; the *Keerthan* must be pleasant, it should not jar on
the ear. If your voice is grating or out of tune, do not
disturb the melody, but, repeat the *Naamaavali* in your
mind. Sing so that the full significance of each Name is
evident to the hearers. Do not repeat each line more than
twice; let there be time during the journey for a variety
of *Naamaavalis* (compilation of divine names) dealing
with many Forms and manifestations of God. Do not
plan to go through distances too long for the party.
Maintain the sacred atmosphere from the first step to
the last.

Devotion must confer peace and joy

Gather in a temple or some holy place, repeat the
Pranava (the sound of *OM*) and *Suprabhaatha* (early
morning serenade) and then, move on for
Nagarasankeerthan. Repeat the Om slowly,
contemplating its vast potentialities. The A emerges
from the throat, the U rolls over the tongue and M
ends on the lips; that is to say, Om which is a
composite of A U and M is the sum and substance of
all the words that can emanate from the human
tongue. It is the primordial, fundamental sound,
symbolic of the Universal Absolute. After the M there
must be the unheard resonance, which represents the
attributeless, formless, Abstract, the *Niraakaara
Parabrahman.* The ascending voice of the *Pranava* or
Om must take a curve at M and descend as slowly as it
rose, taking as much time as when it ascended,
disappearing in the silence, which echoes in the inner
consciousness.

Devotion must confer peace and joy; do not therefore use the *Mandalis* and *Sathsangs* of which you are members to disturb your peace or the peace of others. If you remember that the one goal you must place before you is *Aathma-saakshaathkaara*, and if you enter upon *Saadhana*, then, such tendencies will not develop in you. It is because your aims are worldly, your ideals, material success, fame and authority over others, that you breed discord and doubt among the members. Change your attitudes and outlook. Make your lives worth while. Render the units more useful for all.

All India Conference, 22-11-1969

Some people have their minds and senses like cotton balls and a spark of jnaana will set them ablaze and they achieve victory! Some others have them like dried faggots; they take longer time, but, victory is certain. Most have minds and senses like green fuel and even the raging fire of jnaana may be put out by the onslaught of the moisture contained in them. Make your mind and senses like clean finely ginned cotton.

Sathya Sai Baaba

35. "From me," not "for me"

THE Valedictory Session of this Third All India
Conference is on us, so soon. Time swoops past like a
whirlwind, sweeping everything before it. So one has to
concentrate on the duty of the moment, leaving the
consequence to the God who prompted it and made the
task possible, giving one the chance to carry it out. Time
ticks on relentlessly and man is born, lives, dies, rotating
on the wheel of *Karma* and conse-quence, unaware of the
means of escaping from the oncoming destiny. Agony and
anxiety have not softened his heart; adventure and
achievement have not made him humble. He is proud of his
advance in the path of hatred and haughtiness. He revels in
cruelty and sin. He displays an unholy satisfaction in
immorality and untruth. He has reduced himself to a level
lower than that of beasts.

Man evokes pity because of this plight. For, he has
taken the wrong turn on the road to happiness and landed
himself in this hell. No one seeks grief; all seek only joy.
But, those who know that grief is the interlude between

two joys and joy the interval between two griefs, will seek to attain the stage when they will not be agitated either by the fierce or the friendly storm! That stage of equanimity is the most desirable. It is what is called *Nirvaana*, when the mind is in perfect equilibrium, unaffected by the blows of fortune, good or bad. For, he knows that he has no right to judge, whether what happens is good or bad, beneficial or otherwise.

Saadhana has to enlarge the experience

To reach this stage of Bliss, man must live a life of *saadhana*. If you take one step after another, however short the step, you can walk even a hundred miles! An eagle, however intrepid in flight, has to spread its wings and venture into the wind so that it can reach a few feet away. If the will to step forward or to unfurl the wing is not there, progress is but a fond dream. The *ichchaa-shakthi* (Will Power), has to be sharpened and shaped as an instrument for progress. This individual can fulfil himself only through the service of others, expansion into the universal. *Saadhana* has to enlarge the vision, enhance the experience, and enthuse the *Jeevaathma* (individualised soul) to merge in the *Param-aathma* (Supreme soul). It starts with the question. "What am I contributing to the welfare of my neighbour? Not, what am I collecting from my neighbour?" You can draw cheques on a bank, only when you have deposited therein; or, you can mortgage your property and take a loan; or the bank may grant you an overdraft.

The property on which you can take a loan is the "accumulated merit consequent on the good deeds of previous lives"; the overdraft on which you can draw in times of emergency is Grace, which God showers, when you are sincere and steady enough to deserve it. You must give some surety or something as security, to get a loan; the surety is Divine Grace; the security is the fixing of your

faith, the fullness of your surrender. The security and
the surety can also be the *Guru*, who knows the disciple
and his attainments and possibilities.

But, about the extent of ancestral property,
(accumulated merit), you have no information; you cannot
count on that. Also, you do not know where to get a *Guru* who
will be a reliable surety or an acceptable security. Such are
rare indeed. So, win Grace and earn overdrafts, against a
lean day. That is the best source. The more systematic and
successful your *saadhana*, the more useful you will be for
yourself and society.

Mother is the earliest teacher of the child

Since this is a Conference of Workers engaged in the
practice and promotion of Sathya Sai Ideals, let me dwell upon
a few items of work I feel important at the present juncture.
First, the Sathya Sai *Seva Dhal* (Service corps): All States
must have a common badge, a common curriculum of
spiritual discipline and study, a common course of practical
training in first aid, social service, etc. Now, we have *Seva
Dhals* in Bombay, Madras, Kerala, Andhra and some other
States, but each *Dhal* is being trained without reference to
what is being done in other States.

Second, *Mahila Sathsang* (Women's Club): The Mother
is held as the object of affectionate reverence in Indian Culture. She is the mistress of the house, the earliest teacher
of the child, the person who lovingly transmits the culture
of this ancient land to its heirs in their most formative
years. The mother and the father are the first examples in
social behaviour that the child sees before it and learns to
imitate. They teach *Bhakthi* and *Prapaththi* (adoration of
God and surrender to the Highest); they represent *Shaanthi* and *Prema* (equanimity and love) before the watchful
and receptive eyes of the child. So, they have to be in-

spired to take their share in the spiritual awakening that
this Organisation is embarking upon.

Tolerance and humility have to be promoted in the
rising generation through the promotion of *saadhana*
among the mothers. They are Mother Earth, which ger-
minates the seeds and fosters them into stalwart saplings
and trees. Saline soil stunts the saplings and damages the
crops. Every one has a mother as the source of his life and
body. So the mother has to be strong in mind and body, ripe
in culture and character, sanctified by holy thoughts and
steeped in love and dedication. Good mothers make a good
nation. Mothers have to be repositories of *Thyaaga*, *Yoga*
and *Bhakthi*---sacrifice, discipline and devotion. Their
Karma (activity) must be based on these three urges.

Ease and elevation cannot go together

It is now six years since the *Sai Samithis* (branches) have
been established in this country, in place after place; they
started with very elementary items of work like *Bhajan* and
study of sacred scriptures, but, as each *Samithi* gained
experience through contact with others, the activities have
today become more varied and intensive. After this
Conference, when you go to your places, I want that you should
explore the possibility of expanding the work among mothers,
children and youth. The *Mahila Vibhaag* has to be
strengthened. In places where there are no *Mahila Sathsangs*,
try to start one, and have *Bala Vihaars* under their guidance.

Third, *NagChilarasankeerthan*: There were some
rumblings heard during this Conference that it is rather
hard for office-bearers and members to wake up at 4-30
a.m. and after *Omkaaram* and *Suprabhatham*, walk
about a mile or so, with others singing *Bhajans*! All good
things have to be done the hard way. Ease and elevation
cannot go together. The sages welcome the hard way life;

Kunthi the Queen-Mother of the Paandavas prayed that she may be blessed with a succession of disasters, for they forged her life into a charming chain of prayer. The Lord therefore was ever before her mind's eye. Hardships keep one always alert and in trim. They reveal hidden resources of skill and intelligence; they toughen fortitude and deepen the roots of faith. I am surprised that a request was made to exempt Office-bearers from participation in *Nagarasankeerthan* beyond six *keerthans* a year! And this, from people who attend 600 cinema shows a year. It is a disgrace, that such a proposal was ever brought! Playing cards for hours together perhaps, for such people, is a more sacred rite. Some one raised another objection, against women moving along the streets in the early morning hours! Rather humiliating, they said! Is it not humiliating for these women to stand for hours in queues before cinema houses for a ticket? Or at a bus-stand waiting for a vehicle to come by? No.

Sankeerthan is the highest form of social service

The *keerthan* gives *Aanandha* to the participant and *Aanandha* to the listeners. It is its own reward. It is nothing dishonourable; it is the highest form of social service, and self-help. Do not doubt or hesitate. Even if no one else joins, go alone. You came alone into the world and you go out of it alone. Why then lament when you do not gather companions around you when you do *keerthan* in your village and move from street to street? People may laugh at you, call you insane, question your motives, but persist; they will soon see how happy, how healthy, how holy you are and slowly they will throng around you, on the Godward path. Man and woman, though master and wife, have different spiritual destinies; each has to go at his or her own pace. They may be inter-related and interdependent in secular matters, but, in spiritual matters, each has to carve out his or her own career. Make the home a seat of harmony; then, the village will be a home for concord, the state will be having peace and the nation will be happy, and the world will have prosperity.

When you live the life of *saadhana*, you will meet with opposition from various sources. But, do not attach any importance to such. First, your kith and kin will try to divert you into worldly pursuits. Krishna had his own maternal uncle as his inveterate foe! Raama had a stepmother who sought to exile him into the jungle! Do not be cowed down by cynics or the critics, who may abound in the family. Then there is public opinion, which might decry the spiritual path and subject you to ridicule or worse. Sisupaala, Jaraasandha and the brood of traducers tried hard to smother the mission of the Lord, when he was here as Krishna. Another obstacle is from the worshippers of Names and Forms different from those which you have adopted as most appealing to you. People who are attached to one particular Name and Form, either through hereditary preference or mere fancy are prone to persecute those who adore other Names and Forms. It is far better to die tracking a tiger than live to boast of shooting a lame jackal!

Children have reverence towards knowledge

Women have a great role to play in the moral regeneration of the people. That is the reason for the new emphasis on *Mahila Sathsanghs*. They can tell the children the epic stories of sacrifice and heroism, of saints who sought God and saw Him in Truth, Beauty and Goodness everywhere, of great men and women, who delved into the secrets of the Universe and the Law of all laws, which governs the microcosm and the macrocosm, in equal measure. Christ said, let children come unto me.

They have the sense of wonder, fresh and free; they have the simple, sincere eagerness to know; they have reverence towards knowledge and power. Tell them of Raama, Krishna, Nachiketas, Dhruva, Urmila, Seetha, Hanumaan, Arjuna and many others whom they can picture with admiration in their minds. Indhra Devi said just now that people love their own children and coddle them, but people do not love the children of their neighbours! In fact, the neighbour's children are treated as nuisances. This sense of mine and thine stands as a barrier between spiritual progress and the individual.

The Divine is the inner core of all beings, near and far, big or small. Expand your consciousness to its uttermost limits. Really speaking, it has no limits at all. This cannot be done on an instalment plan, or on a cash-down basis! No. It is possible only through an inner transformation, through *dhyaana, japa,* or *Naamasmarana,* in the constant contemplation of the Supreme majesty that is in you. Once you reveal to yourself that Majesty, you can be an effective instrument for service and uplift, among the depressed and the distressed around you. The Divine sprouts in the heart, grows in the Consciousness and blooms in all the mental and physical activities of man. Now the Divine Principle is beyond your experience, because you are not ready to give your best to others, who also contain the self-same Principle. When you are ready to give, you are entitled to take; not until then.

We find that, even among the highly educated, the I.A.S. men and I.P.S. men, etc., very few help their aged parents, very few try to give them at least a fraction of the comforts they themselves command. Each one is immersed in ensuring his own standard of living. How long is he to stay in that standard? A day will come when he has to bid farewell to all that he has garnered with cunning and cleverness, inflicting pain and sorrow, discontent and distress on many. Service to parents, elders and the suffering gives joy and satisfaction to all concerned. Virtue and righteousness---these will bear witness on your behalf, on the Day of Judgement; neither your bank account nor your income tax returns will speak on your behalf.

Let me end on this note: Do not waver, hesitate or doubt your destiny. Yearn to realise your Reality; that yearning itself will endow you with steady endeavour and the Grace of God which will remove all obstacles. Be an example to others. Do not scatter advice, without the authority born of practical experience. Do not search for the faults of others; seek your own. Love, co- operate, help, serve. That is your prime duty, as leaders of the Sathya Sai Units in your villages.

All India Conference, Prashaanthi Nilayam,
22-11-1969

Bhakthi cannot come into man from outside him; it has to be grown from within by an effort to cleanse the mind, to know the nature and origin of man and the universe, to grasp the relation of man with all the external objects which now fascinate and foil him.

Sathya Sai Baaba

Glossary

Meanings of Sanskrit words used in discussing religious and philosophical topics, more particularly used in the discourses by Sri Sathya Sai Baba, reproduced in this volume, are given in this glossary. While the English equivalents for the Sanskrit words have been given in the text with reference to the context, this glossary attempts to provide comprehensive meanings and detailed explanations of the more important Sanskrit words, for the benefit of lay readers who are interested in Hindu religion and philosophy.

Aakaasa - Space; ether; the subtlest form of matter.

Aanandha - Divine bliss. The Self is unalloyed, eternal bliss. Pleasures are but its faint and impermament shadows.

Aaraadhana - Divine service; propitiation.

Ashrama Dharma - The life of a Hindu cosists of four stages as *aashramas. Aashrama Dharma* is the code of disciplines laid down for the blossoming of spiritual consciousness during the four stages---*Brahmachaari* (the student celibrate), *Grihastha* (householder), *Vaana-Prastha* (the recluse in the forest), and the *sanyaasin* (the ascetic or the monk).

Aasthika - One who believes in God, scriptures and the *Guru.*

Aathma - Self; Soul. Self, with limitations, is *jeeva* (the individual soul). Self, with no limitations, is *Brahman* (the Supreme Reality).

Aathma jnaana - Knowledge of the Self which is held out as the Supreme goal of human endeavour.

Aathmaswarupam - Self embodied; of the nature of Self. The real man in us is the Self which is pure consciousness!

Aathma thatwa - Principle of the Self; the truth or the essential nature of the Self.

Abhayaswarupam - Fearlessness embodied; of the nature of fearlessness. *Brahman* is fearless.

Adhwaitha - Non-dualism. The philosophy of absolute oneness of God, soul and Universe.

Aham Brahmaasmi - "I am *Brahman*". This is one of the great *Vedhic* dicta (*Mahaa Vaakyaas*).

Ahamkaara - Egotism resulting from the identification of one's self with the body. It causes the sense of "I do" and "I experience".

Ajnaana - Ignorance (which prevents perception of the Reality).

Annamaya kosa - Material or gross sheath of the soul; the physical body.

Antharyaamin - Inner Motivator or Controller. (God is described thus because He resides in all beings and controls them from within).

Archana - Ritual worship of a deity, making offerings with recitation of manthras and holy names.

Avathaar - Incarnation of God. Whenever there is a decline of *Dharma*, God comes down to the world assuming bodily form to protect the good, punish the wicked and re-establish *Dharma*. An *Avathaar* is born and lives free and is ever conscious of His mission. By His precept and example, He opens up new paths in spirituality, shedding His grace on all.

Bhaagavatham - A sacred book composed by Sage Vyasa dealing with Vishnu and His incarnations, especially Shri Krishna.

Bhagavat-thatwam - The truth or essential nature of the Lord.

Bhajana - Congregational chant group worship by devotees with devotional music in which repetition of holy names predominates.

Bhaktha - Principle of God head. A devotee who has intense selfless love for God.

Bhakthi - Devotion to God; intense selfless love for God.

Bhavasaagaram - Ocean of worldly life. The worldly life of a being is considered to be the ocean which he has to cross and reach the other side for liberation from the cycle of birth and death.

Bhoga - Enjoyment; experience; the antithesis of *yoga*.

Bodha - Perception; knowledge; consciousness.

Buddhi - Intellect; intelligence; faculty of discrimination.

Brahma - The Creator; the First of the Hindu Trinity.

Brahmaandam - The Cosmic egg, the Universe.

Brahmachaari - A celibate student who lives with and learns from his spiritual guide.

Brahman - The Supreme Being; the Absolute Reality; Impersonal God with no form or attributes. The uncaused cause of the Universe; Existence - Consciousness-Bliss Absolute (*Sath-chith-aanandha*); The Eternal Changeless Reality, not conditioned by time, space and causation.

Dhama - Self-control; restraining the sense organs which run after sense objects seeking pleasure. This is an important discipline for an aspirant practising *yoga*.

Dharma - Righteousness; religion; code of duties; duty; essential nature of a being or thing. It holds together the entire Universe. Man is exhorted to practise *Dharma* to achieve material and spiritual welfare. The *Vedhas* contain the roots of *Dharma*. God is naturally interested in the reign of *Dharma*.

Dhyaana - Meditation; an unbroken flow of thought towards the object of concentration. It steadies and stills the mind and makes it fit for realisation in course of time.

Dhwaitha - Dualism; the doctrine that the individual and the Supreme Soul are two distinct principles.

Gaayathri manthra - The very sacred *Vedhic* prayer for self-enlightenment repeated piously at dawn, noon and twilight devotions.

Guna - Quality, property, trait; one of the three constituents of Nature (*Saathwa, Rajas and Thamas*). They bind the soul to the body. Man's supreme goal in life is to transcend the *gunas* and attain liberation from the cycle of birth and death.

Guru - Spiritual guide; a knower of *Brahman*, who is calm, desireless, merciful and ever ready to help and guide the spiritual aspirants who approach him.

Hridhayaakasha - Space in the (spiritual) heart in which the Self is imagined in meditation and prayer.

Ishta devatha - The chosen deity through which a devotee contemplates on God.

Ishwara - The Supreme Ruler; the Personal God; He is *Brahman* associated with *Maayaa* but has it under His control unlike the *jeeva* who is *Maayaa*'s slave. He has a lovely form, auspicious attributes and infinite power to create, sustain and destroy. He dwells in the heart of every being, controlling it from within. He responds positively to true devotion and sincere prayer.

Japam - Pious repetition of holy name or sacred manthra, practised as a spiritual discipline.

Jeeva/Jeevaathma - The individual soul in a state of non- realisation of its identity with Brahman. It is the self-deluded, bound spirit unaware of its own true nature. It is subjected to sensations of pain and pleasure, birth and death, etc.

Jnaana - Sacred knowledge; knowledge of the spirit, pursued as a means to Self-realisation. It is direct experience of God, as the Soul of the souls. *Jnaanam* makes a man omniscient, free, fearless and immortal.

Jnaani - A sage possessing *Jnaanam* (unitive spiritual knowledge and experience).

Kaarana sariram - Causal body which carries the impressions and tendencies in seed state. It is the sheath of bliss; the innermost of the five sheaths of the soul.

Karma - Action; deed; work; religious rite; the totality of innate tendencies formed as a consequence of acts done in previous lives. Every *karma* produces a lasting impression on the mind of the doer, apart from affecting others. Repetition of a particular *karma* produces a tendency (*vaasana*) in the mind. *Karma* is of three kinds: (i) *Praarabdha* : which is being exhausted in the present life: (ii) *Aagami* : which is being accumulated in the present life, and *(iii) Samchita*, which is stored to be experienced in future lives. *Akarma* is action that is done without any intention to gain the consequences; *Vikarma* is action that is intentionally done.

Koshas - The five sheaths enclosing the soul---sheaths of bliss, intelligence, mind, vital energy and physical matter.

Kshathriya - A member of the warrior caste, one of the four social groups (*varnas*) of the Hindu community.

Kshethra - Field; the body in which the *jeeva* reaps the harvest of his *karma*.

Kshetragna - The Knower of the field; the Spirit; the individual knowing Self.

Leela - Sport; play; the Universe is viewed as Divine sport or play.

Lingam - Sign; symbol.

Linga sariram - The subtle body with its vital principles, subtle organs, mind, intellect and ego. When the gross body dies, the self departs, clothed in the subtle body.

Loka - Any of the 14 worlds (visible and invisible) inhabited by living beings.

Maayaa - The mysterious, creative and delusive power of *Brahman* through which God projects the appearance of the Universe.

Maayaa is the material cause and *Brahman* is the efficient cause of the Universe. *Brahman* and *Maayaa* are inextricably associated with each other like fire and its power to heat. *Maayaa* deludes the *Jeevas* in egoism, making them forget their true spiritual nature.

Mahaabhaaratha - The Hindu epic composed by Sage Vyaasa which deals with the deeds and fortunes of the cousins (the Kauravas and Paandavaas) of the Lunar race, with Lord Krishna playing a significant and decisive role in shaping the events. The *Bhagavadgeeitha* and Vishnu Sahasranama occur in this great epic. It is considered to be the Fifth *Vedha* by the devout Hindus. Of this great epic, it is claimed that "what is not in it is nowhere".

Manas - Mind, the inner organ which has four aspects: (i) *Manas* (Mind) which deliberates, desires and feels; (ii) *Buddhi*, (intellect) that understands, reasons and decides; (iii) *Ahamkaara*, (*'I'* sense) and (iv) *Chitha* - (memory). The Mind with all its desires and their broods, conceals the divinity within man. Purification of the mind is essential for realisation of the Self.

Maanava - Man, descendent of Manu, the law-giver.

Manomaya-kosha - Mental sheath. One of the five sheaths enclosing the soul. It consists of the mind and the five subtle sensory organs. It is endowed with the power of will.

Manthra - A sacred formula, mystic syllable or word symbol uttered during the performance of the rituals or meditation. They represent the spiritual truths directly revealed to the *Rishis* (seers). The section of the *Vedha* which contains these hymns (*manthras*) is called the *Samhitha*.

Moksha/Mukthi - Liberation from all kinds of bondage, especially the one to the cycle of birth and death. It is a state of absolute freedom, peace and bliss, attained through Self-realisation. This is the supreme goal of human endeavour, the other three being, *dharma* (righteousness), *artha* (wealth and power) and *kaama* (sense-pleasure).

Naamasmarana - Remembering God through His Name; one of the important steps of spiritual discipline (*saadhana*) to obtain God's grace and to make progress in the spiritual journey.

Nididhyaasana - Concentration on the truth about the Self after hearing it (*sravana*) from the *guru* and reflecting on it (*manana*). It is thus the third step on the Path of Knowledge (*Jnaana-Yoga*).

Nivrithi Maarga - The path of renunciation that demands giving up desires and concentrating on God. The *Upanishadhs* which form the *Jnaana-kanda* (the section dealing with unitive spiritual knowledge) of the *Vedhas*, deal with this path. This path is opposed to the *pravrithi marga* (the path of desire) which worldly men pursue, seeking the good things here and hereafter.

Praanamaya kosha - Sheath of vital energy. It consists of five vital principles and five subtle organs of action. It is endowed with the power of action.

Prakrithi - Nature; the Divine Power of Becoming; also known as *Maayaa, Avidhya* and *Shakthi;* the world of matter and mind as opposed to the Spirit. *Prakrithi* has three dispositions or *gunas* (*sathwa, rajas,* and *tamas*) that go into the make-up of all living and non-living beings in the Universe, in varying proportions leading to the appearance of infinite multiplicity in form, nature and behaviour.

Pranava - *Om*; the sacred seed-sound and symbol of *Brahman*; "the most exalted syllable in *Vedhas*". It is used in meditation on God. It is uttered first before a *Vedhic manthra* is chanted.

Prema - Ecstatic love of God; (divine love of the most intense kind).

Puuja - Ritual worship in which a deity is invoked in an idol or picture and propitiated as a Royal Guest with offerings of flowers, fruits and other eatables along with recitation of appropriate *manthras* and show of relevant signs.

Puranaas - The Hindu *Shaasthras* (scriptures) in which *Vedhic* truths are illustrated through tales of divine incarnations and heroes. Sage Vyaasa is believed to have written them. Of the 18 *Puranaas*, Srimad *Bhaagavatha* is the best known.

Raamaayana - This sacred Hindu epic composed by Sage Valmeeki deals with the incarnation of Vishnu as Shri Raama who strove all his life to reestablish the reign of *Dharma* in the world. The *Raamaayana* has played a very important role in influencing and shaping the Hindu ethos over the centuries.

Rajas/Rajo Guna - One of the three *gunas* (qualities or dis-positions) of *Maayaa* or *Prakrithi*. *Rajas* is the quality of passion, energy, restlessness, attachment and extroversion. It results in pain.

Thaapam - Pain, misery; distress caused by the three types of agencies (*thaapathrayam*). The agencies are *aadhyaadmika* (diseases and disturbances of body and mind); *aadhi bhowthika* (other beings); and *aadhi deivikam* (supernatural agencies like storm, floods, earthquakes, planets, etc).

Thamas - One of the *gunas* (qualities and dispositions) of *Maayaa* or *Prakrithi*. It is the quality of dullness, inertia, darkness and tendency to evil. It results in ignorance.

Saadhana - Spiritual discipline or effort aimed at God realisation. The *saadhaka* (aspirant) uses the spiritual discipline to attain the goal of realisation.

Samaadhi - It is the super-conscious state transcending mind and intellect, attained through rigorous and pro Saadhana. In that state of consciousness, the objective world and the ego vanish and the Reality is perceived or communed with, in utter peace and bliss. When in this state, the aspirant realises his oneness with God, it is called *Nirvikalpa Samaadhi*.

Samsaara - Wordly life; life of the *jiva* through repeated births and deaths. Liberation means getting freed from this cycle.

Sanaathana Dharma - Eternal religion. A descriptive term for what has come to be called Hinduism. It has no single founder or text of its own. It is more a commonwealth of religious faiths and a way of life.

Saamanya Dharma - Code of conduct common to all persons in any one social group.

Shaasthras - The Hindu scriptures containing the teachings of the *rishis*. The *Vedhas*, the *Upanishadhs*, the *Ithihassas* (epics), the *Puranaas* and the *Smrithis* (codes of conduct), etc., form the *Shaasthras* of the Hindus. They teach us how to live wisely and well with all the tenderness and concern of the Mother.

Sathwa - One of the three *gunas* (qualities and dispositions) of *Maayaa* or *Prakrithi*. It is the quality of purity, brightness, peace and harmony. It leads to knowledge. Man is exhorted to overcome *thamas* by *rajas*, and *rajas* by *sathwa* and finally to go beyond *sathwa* itself to attain liberation.

Sthitha prajna - A man of realisation with a steady, tranquil and cheerful mind ever dwelling on God. He is a man of self-control, even-minded in all circumstances and totally free from all selfish desires. After death he attains freedom from *Samsaara*.

Swadharma - One's *dharma* or duty that accords with one's nature. This is an important concept in the Gita.

Upaasana - Worship or contemplation of God.

Upanishadh - The very sacred portions of the *Vedhas* that deal with God, man and universe, their nature and interrelationships. Spiritual knowledge (*jnaana*) is their content. So they form the *Jnaana Kaanda* of the *Vedhas*.

Vairaagya - Detachment; desire and ability to give up all transitory enjoyments.

Varna dharma - The Hindu community is divided into four *varnas* (social groups), based on *gunas* and vocations. *Braahmana* (the Custodian of spiritual and moral role), *Kshathriya* (the warrior gray which rules and defends the land), *Vaishya* (the group dealing with commerce, business and trade) *Shuudhra* (the group devoted to labour and service to the community). Each varna has its own *dharma* (*varna dharma*) restrictions and regulations that strive to canalise his impulses and instinct into fields that are special to his place in society, controls pertaining to the duties cast upon

Vedhas - The oldest and the holiest of the Hindu scriptures, the primary source of authority in Hindu religion and philosophy. They are four in number --- the Rig Vedha, Saama Vedha, Yajur Vedha and Atharva Vedha.

Vedhaantha - Means "the end of the *Vedhas*". It is the essence of the *Vedhas* enshrined in the *Upanishadhs*. The philosophy of non-dualism, or qualified non-dualism, or dualism based on the *Upanishadhic* teachings, is denoted by this term.

Vishesha Dharma - Code of conduct to be observed in special situations; obligations to be discharged on special occasions, or when faced with special situations.

Vijnaanamaya kosha - One of the five *koshas* (sheaths) of the soul. It consists of intellect and the five subtle sense organs. It is endowed with the power to know. The "I" or subject of experience or action is seated here.

Viveka - Discrimination; the reasoning by which one realises what is real and permanent and what is non-real and impermanent.

Vriththi Dharma - The moral code that regulates and enriches a person's profession.

Yagna - A *Vedhic* rite or sacrifice. Any self-denying act of service in the name of God.

Yoga - Means union with God, as also the path by which this union of the soul with God is achieved. The four important paths of *Yoga* are those of knowledge, action, meditation and devotion.

PUBLICATIONS IN ENGLISH

PRICE

	Rs. P.
Vahini Series (Books Written by Baghavan Sri Sathya Sai Baba)	
Bhagavatha Vahini (The Story of the Glory of the Lord)	17.50
Dharma Vahini (The Path of Virtue)	8.00
Dhyana Vahini (Practice Of Meditation)	8.50
Geetha Vahini (The Divine Gospel)	15.50
Jnaana Vahini (The Stream of Eternal Wisdom)	7.50
Leela Kaivalya Vahini (The Cosmic Play Of God)	5.50
Prashaanthi Vahini (The Bliss of Supreme Peace)	7.50
Prasnothara Vahini (Answers To Spiritual Questions)	8.50
Prema Vahini (The Stream of Divine Love)	9.50
Rama Katha Rasa Vahini I (The Sweet Story of Rama's Glory)	19.00
Rama Katha Rasa Vahini II (The Sweet Story of Rama's Glory)	14.50
Sandeha Nivarini (Clearance of Spiritual Doubts)	13.50
Sathya Sai Vahini (Spiritual Message of Sathya Sai)	15.00
Sutra Vahini (Analytical Aphorisms on Supreme Reality)	8.00
Upanishad Vahini (Essence of Vedhic Knowledge)	9.50
Vidya Vahini (Flow of Spiritual Education)	8.00

Sathya Sai Speaks Series (Discourses By Bhagavan Sri Sathya Sai Baba)

Sathya Sai Speaks (Revised & Enlarged)	VOL. I	(Year 1953 to 1960)	Under Print
Sathya Sai Speaks (Revised & Enlarged)	VOL. II	(Year 1961 & 1962)	27.50
Sathya Sai Speaks (Revised & Enlarged)	VOL. III	(Year 1963)	24.00
Sathya Sai Speaks (Revised & Enlarged)	VOL. IV	(Year 1964)	27.50
Sathya Sai Speaks (Revised & Enlarged)	VOL. V	(Year 1965)	26.00
Sathya Sai Speaks (Revised & Enlarged)	VOL. VI	(Year 1966)	22.00

Sathya Sai Speaks (Revised & Enlarged)	VOL. VII	(Year 1967)	24.00
Sathya Sai Speaks (Revised & Enlarged)	VOL. VIII	(Year 1968)	Under print
Sathya Sai Speaks (Revised & Enlarged)	VOL. IX	(Year 1969)	20.50
Sathya Sai Speaks (Revised & Enlarged)	VOL. X	(Year 1970)	26.00
Sathya Sai Speaks (Revised & Enlarged)	VOL. XI	(Year 1971-72)	Under print
Sathya Sai Speaks (Revised & Enlarged)	VOL. XII	(Year 1973-74)	Under print
Sathya Sai Speaks (Revised & Enlarged)	VOL. XIII	(Year 1975-77)	Under print
Sathya Sai Speaks (Revised & Enlarged)	VOL. XIV	(Year 1978-80)	Under print
Sathya Sai Speaks (Revised & Enlarged)	VOL. XV	(Year 1981-82)	28.00

Sathyam Sivam Sundaram Series
(Life Story of Bhagavan Sri Sathya Sai Baba))

Sathyam Sivam Sundaram	Part I (Birth to 1962)	16.50
Sathyam Sivam Sundaram	Part II (Years 1962 to 1968)	15.50
Sathyam Sivam Sundaram	Part III (Years 1969 to 1972)	16.00
Sathyam Sivam Sundaram	Part IV (Years 1973 to 1979)	14.00

Summer Showers Series (Discourses on Indian
Culture & Spirituality By Bhagavan Sri Sathya Sai Baba)

Summer Showers in Brindavan	1972	15.50
Summer Showers in Brindavan	1973	15.50
Summer Showers in Brindavan	1974	17.50
Summer Roses on the Blue Mountains	1976	14.50
Summer Showers in Brindavan	1977	17.50
Summer Showers in Brindavan	1978	13.50
Summer Showers in Brindavan	1979	14.50
Summer Showers in Brindavan	1990	17.00

Children's Books

Stories for Children Part I	--	---	11.50
Stories for Children Part II	--	---	12.00
Chinna Katha	--	---	16.00
My Life Is My Message	--	---	14.00

Other Books

Africa for Sai Baaba --By Dare Ogunkolati	--	3.50
Conversations with Bhagavan Sri Sathya Sai Baba		
Dr. John S. Hislop	--	12.50
Divine Memories of Sathya Sai Baba --		
Diana Baskin	--	31.00
Eashwaramma (The Chosen Mother of		
Bhagavan Sri Sathya Sai Baba)	---	13.00
Finding God -- By Charles Penn	---	34.00
Garland of 108 Precious Gems		
(108 Holy names of Bhagavan)	---	11.00
My Baaba and I -- By Dr. John S. Hislop	---	26.00
My Beloved -- By Charles Penn	---	25.00
Namasmarana	---	5.50
Prashaanthi -- Pathway to Peace	---	10.00
Saadhana -- The Inward Path	---	14.50
Sai Baba The Holy Man & The Psychiatrist --		
Dr.Samuel H. Sandweiss	---	36.00
Sai Baba the Ultimate Experience -- By Phyllis Krystal		29.00
Sai Ram -- By Charles Penn	---	25.00
Sathya Sai-Education in Human Values	---	16.00
Sathya Sai-Golden Jubilee Book of Thoughts		
(Calendar)	---	20.00
Sathya Sai Baba --- God Incarnate - Vol II--By Victor Kanu		23.00
Sathya Sai Lyrics --- By Dr. V.K. Gokak	---	7.50
Sathya Sai --- The Eternal Charioteer		35.00
Spirit and the Mind -- By Dr. Samuel H. Sandweiss	---	31.00
Loving God - By N. Kasturi	...	30.00

MISCELLANEOUS

Bhajanavali	---	4.00
Shirdi To Puttaparthi --- By Dr. R.T. Kakade	---	30.00
Guide to Indian Culture and Spirituality	---	6.00
Daily Prayers to Bhagavan	---	6.00
Divine Guidelines for Bal Vikas	---	10.00
Sai Baba Avathar --- By Howard Murphet	---	40.00
Sai Baba-Invitation to Glory --- Howard Murphet	---	33.00
Sai Baba-Man of Miracles --- By Howard Murphet	---	36.00
Sathya Sai - The Avathaar of Love	---	50.00

INLAND/OVERSEAS BOOK ORDERS

Books are despatched only by Registered Post and not by V.P.P., subject to availability, when indents and remittance are received by Money Order/International Money Order/Cheques Account Payee or Account Payee Bank Draft in favour of **The Convenor, Sri Sathya Sai Books and Publications Trust, Prasanthi Nilayam, Anantapur District, Andra Pradesh, India, Pin Code 515134.**

POSTAGE (Inland) :

At the rate of 50 paise per 100 gms: For an order of

3 to 5 books (Approximately 1 kg)   Postage Rs. 5/- plus
             Registration Rs. 6/-
             Total Rs. 11/-,

6 to 9 books (Approximately 2 kgs.) Postage Rs. 10/- plus
             Registration Rs. 6/-
             Total Rs. 16/-.)

PACKAGE IS FREE : While remitting - Please Calculate cost of books indented plus postage plus Registration Charges.

Postage (Overseas)   :   For 6 books or less (approx. 2 kg.)

SEA MAIL DESPATCH   :   Rs. 74/- (Including Postal Registration charges) for each 2 Kg. or less packet. (US $ 3 Pound Sterling 2).

AIR MAIL DESPATCH   :   Rs. 375/- (Including Postal Registration charges) for each 2 Kg. or less packet. US $ 14 or Pound Sterling 8.

NOTES